WARRIOR
WISDOM

IN ONE MONTH

ARRANGED IN DAILY READINGS

Jim Wagner

Training for a violent world.

JIM WAGNER

REALITY-BASED
PERSONAL PROTECTION

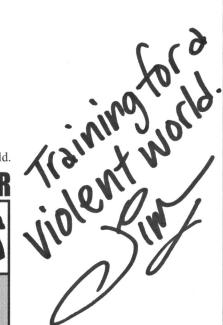

WARRIOR WISDOM IN ONE MONTH

Copyright © 2018 by Jim Wagner

Published by **WAR**Arts
www.jimwagnerrealitybased.com

ISBN: 978-0-993358-7-2

Printed in the United States of America

The Four Square RBPP logo (fist, gun, grenade, & knife) is a trademark (TM)

The *Training for a violent world.* motto is a trademark (TM)

Cover photos (from left to right): 1) That's me at 17 years old when I was a student of Dan Inosanto studying Bruce Lee's Jeet Kune Do system. 2) I was on my police department's S.W.A.T. team, and then trained tactical teams when I was a sergeant with the Sheriff's Department. 3) I was a police officer on patrol. 3) I was a sergeant in a Military Police unit, and a Terrorism Liaison Officer (TLO).

WARNING: This book is FOR INFORMATION ONLY. Neither the publisher nor the author is repsonsible for the use, or the misuse, of the information contained in this book. It is recommended that a physician be consulted before attempting any physical exercise or self-defense training. Initial self-defense training should be done under the strict supervision of a professional instructor. All local, national, and international laws must be obeyed concerning self-defense training, and any use-of-force (threats, injuries and/or death) situation where techniques or tactics are applied.

TABLE OF CONTENTS

Introduction

What is your definition of wisdom? It's a word that has recently fallen out of use in our society. In fact, wisdom is harder to find in individuals today. Wisdom is not just knowing a bunch of facts, but understanding facts in their context (insight), and the ability to use those facts to problem solve in order to achieve a positive outcome. Now, place the word "warrior" in front of the word "wisdom," and you easily conclude the meaning of the term; *it's the ability to use your knowledge, techniques, and tactics to avoid or survive a conflict.*

However, the word "conflict" is a rather big word that can have many meanings. Have you ever had to fight for your lunch money on the school-yard? That's one type of conflict. Have you ever had someone want to go to blows with you because you accidently bumped into them? That's another type of conflict. How about someone lunging at you with a knife or firing a gun at you? Even worse, have you ever been in the middle of a terrorist attack? Has a killer drone ever taken a dive at you? As you can see, nobody can possibly experience every type of fight, therefore you will always lack knowledge and experience in some areas of combat.

No matter what your level of training and experience may be when it comes to self-defense, there is always room to obtain more wisdom. This is exactly why I have written this book. I believe that my diverse background in human conflict will add to what you already know, although I may add a different perspective, and it will fill in some of the gaps that may be missing from your training and experience. In the process you, a warrior (if not actually, then at least at heart), will gain wisdom.

About me before we get started

What qualifies me to impart wisdom, warrior wisdom no less, upon you? It's a legitimate question, and one that should be asked. After all, the study of self-defense is serious business since your safety, or your very life, may depend upon the information, techniques, and tactics you receive from me. Therefore, it is imperative that you know a little something about my background before reading this book. In fact, you should always scrutinize a self-defense instructor's background before embracing their teachings to determine if what they have to offer you is theory they picked up somewhere or battle tested reality. In other words, would the professionals accept the teachings of the instructor you are interested in learning from? And, by "professionals" I mean law enforcement officers, combat military personnel, private security officers, bodyguards, bouncers, et cetera (basically, those who actually fight for a living).

Most people who study the martial arts study one or two systems; maybe three, tops. Most people who join the military stay in one branch of the service, and have no idea what the other branches of the Armed Forces are like; not from actual experience anyway. Most people who earn a badge from a law enforcement agency, which is no easy task I might add, stay with that one agency until retirement. First, they don't want to lose their seniority that took years to get. Second, because they don't want to go back to pulling graveyard shifts again; that's for the younger guys and gals. I've been very fortunate. No, a better word to use is "blessed," because, "I've lived 100 lives," and as such I have gained more wisdom as a warrior than humanly possible.

Yes, of course, I'm joking about living one hundred lives, and I certainly don't believe in reincarnation, but it certainly feels like I have lived that many lives. I've kicked up the sand on a Mediterranean beach training Israeli soldiers how to survive hand-to-hand combat. I've been dripping wet with sweat in the jungles of Argentina teaching Special Forces operators how to raid a terrorist compound. I pulled a suspected Pakistani terrorist off of a fully loaded passenger plane bound for Washington, D.C. I had a prisoner try to kill me in his jail cell. It felt surreal dangling from the end of a rope from a U.S. Marine UH-1 helicopter 500 feet off of the deck, and in "another life" standing on the back of the lowered ramp of a U.S. Air Force C-130 flying nap of the earth to drop supplies with battled hardened Rangers. I froze my butt off sleeping in a lean-two in a German forest enduring a wilderness survival course. I lasted only 15 minutes inside a steamy sauna with a bunch of naked Helsinki police officers after a day of training in the dead of dark winter. I've wiped the dust from my eyes at a live-fire shooting range in the African savanna. In my Army Green Service uniform I stood saluting the President of the United States of America in the Oval Office. I was once imbedded with a riot police unit with the London Metropolitan Police swarming hooligans, and only months later I found myself deep under the murky waters of the Port of Los Angeles in SCUBA gear searching for possible limpet mines on a warship. I've been shot at, stabbed at, punched at, spit at, and accused of being a spy, followed up by a threat to be executed in the Arab country of Jordan. On and on it goes. So, now you know what I mean when I say, "I've lived 100 lives."

As far my rather bold sentence "gaining more wisdom as a warrior than humanly possible," it's not intended to be taken as a braggart. It's just that I have picked up more warrior wisdom along this wild journey of mine than most. I've mastered a dozen martial arts systems. I have worn a shield for a municipal police department, a six-pointed star for a county sheriff, and an eagle topped federal badge for the U.S. government. I've been a combat soldier at the lowest rank in the U.S. Army, a private, all the way up to a Master Sergeant in charge of the Security Forces on a major military base. Over the years my duties have included patrolling gang infested neighborhoods, bicycle patrol at the most posh shopping mall in the United States, a member on the S.W.A.T. team, teaching kids to stay off of drugs, dignitary protection, patrol field supervisor, anti-terrorism, counterterrorism, hand-to-hand combat instructor, firearms instructor, team leader of a military Special Response Team, HOOAH! and some not-so-exciting admin jobs to gain management experience.

I never set out to get all of this training and experience; it's just that one thing led to another. When people are impressed with my long resume, sometimes even to the point of disbelief that one person could have done it all, I often joke, "I had no choice but to learn all this high-speed low-drag stuff, because I always got into trouble with the agency I was with, and I had to move onto the next one." Well, this statement is 99% true. I think I only avoided trouble with one agency in my career. For the rest, when I say "trouble," it was always the type of trouble that resulted from my uncompromising commitment to my safety or those I commanded, and most paper-pushers don't like push back. And so, as a result of my sordid past I couldn't help but pick up a lot of warrior wisdom like a bee having pollen cling to it flying from flower to flower.

I've never seen myself as a "super cop" or a "super soldier." It sometimes takes me a few tries at something to get it right, and I have made my fair share of mistakes out in the field; a few that have almost cost me my life. Having trained with, and having trained extensively, various U.S. Marines units for nine years have I always considered myself a "quiet professional," like the instructor cadre at the 1st Marine Division Scout Sniper School. A quiet professional is someone who knows they don't know everything, and who is constantly absorbing bits of information and wisdom from other warriors in order to learn and improve their own warcraft. The good news is that I have never kept my martial, "war," knowledge to myself. I openly share what I know with my students, save that information that various governments have made me take an oath never to reveal.

The reading of Warrior Wisdom makes you my student by default. Just by reading one topic a day you will continue to gain warrior wisdom. Of course, it is by no means an exhaustive list of everything you need to know, but it is a starting point.

Oh, and one more thing before we get started. At the end of each day I will end with the motto of my Jim Wagner Realtiy-Based Personal Protection system, and that is **Training for a violent world**.

"Training for a violent world" means being prepared for anything from the proverbial bar fight, an "ego fight," to a "life and death fight," like surviving an armed robbery or a terrorist attack. Abiding by this motto does not mean that you are paranoid. Far from it. Are you "paranoid" when you drive a car? Of course not. You drive defensively in order to keep safe. You know full well that if a ball rolls out into the street that you had better stop, because a child is likely to follow. You also pay attention to the car in the lane next to you when you are driving down the road, because you know that there's a possibility that he or she will suddenly change into your lane without signaling. You're ready to act instantly to avoid a collision. Training for a violent world is exactly like defensive driving, in the sense that you are more aware of what to look for when it comes to potential violence. Therefore, at the end of each day I am simply reminding you, reinforcing, this point that you must never forget.

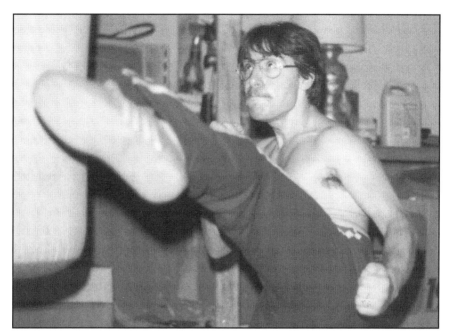

Alfonso Uceda was my first martial arts instructor, and taught me Tae Kwon Do in 1975. He was wise enough to encourage me to study other systems a year later.

From 1976 to 1979 I studied Karate, Judo, Kung-fu, Kenpo, European fencing, Bruce Lee's system Jeet Kune Do, Filipino Kali, Wing Chun, and kickboxing.

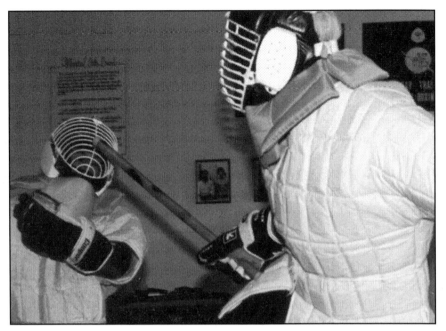

That's me on the right, fighting full contact with sticks, to test out some new safety equipment for my instructor Dan Inosanto at the Filipino Kali Academy.

I started my self-defense teaching career in 1980 when I was in the U.S. Army. I taught private lessons to fellow soldiers who wanted to learn my mixed systems.

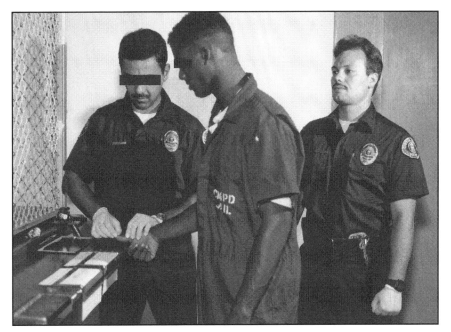

I became a corrections officer in December of 1988. At that time in history we did not carry any weapons, and getting into fights with criminals was a real education.

In early 1990 the Costa Mesa Police S.W.A.T. team allowed me to form a "terrorist cell" as an Opposing Force (OPFOR) for their training sessions. I had 10 members.

I graduated from the police academy on June 21, 1991 and the next day I was on the streets as a patrol officer. Here I am arresting a woman for possession of drugs.

From March 11, 1994 to May 24, 1997 I served on the S.W.A.T. team. This is me during Entry Team training in a Shoot House. Obviously, this is a dry-fire run.

I trained U.S. Marines at Camp Pendleton for years, and in return the instructor cadre allowed me to participate in many courses, like this HRST helicopter course.

These are Iranian Airborne soldiers. Actually, they are role players with the U.S. Army 19th Special Forces. On February 12-13, 1995 I put together their training.

Here I am in a UH-60 Black Hawk helicopter flying over Big Bear, California with U.S. Customs Aviation Operations. You can see the trees passing by in the window.

This is me (center) with my Tactical Swimmer team recapturing a GOPLAT (Gas & Oil Platform) from "terrorists" off of the coast of California for annual training.

I'm proudly standing with my instructors and my classmates after graduating Advanced Sniper Course at the U.S. Marine Scout Sniper School at Camp Pendleton.

On June 13, 2000 I was promoted to the rank of sergeant (Orange County Sheriff's Department), and assigned as the Team Leader of the Dignitary Protection Unit.

Twice the German government flew me out to Saint Augustine, Germany to train their national counterterrorist team Grenzschutzgruppe 9, best known as GSG9.

I'm posing here (bottom left) in Mexico with my S.W.A.T. students of the Grupo Especial Rosarito. A few months later I went back to train other police agencies.

The Helsinki police officer on the left is using my original Criminal Chemical Attack Defense technique. The "attacker" is spraying him with pepper spray.

I was imbedded with the London Metropolitan Police South T.S.G. (riot unit), and I helped suppress rioting hooligans after a soccer match with 160 other Bobbies.

After the terrorist attacks against the United States on September 11, 2001 I joined the Global War on Terrorism as an agent with the U.S. Federal Air Marshal Service.

20

That's me in 2003 teaching the Israeli Army's newest recruits at the Wingate Institute, Bahad 8 (8 בה"ד), which is a fitness and hand-to-hand combat military base.

My battle buddy and I show off our lean-two during a wilderness survival course taught by German Special Forces instructors near the Pfullendorf military base.

Here I am teaching a S.W.A.T. defensive tactics course to operators in Boston. *Train as you fight*, is exactly why they are all in uniform, and with full gear on.

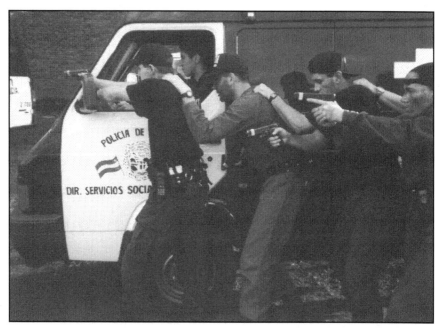

Argentina faced radical Islamic terrorism, and this is why I was flown down there; to teach them techniques and tactics. Here are some of my students in Misiones.

In 2006 I went back into the military as a Reserve soldier. In this photo I am in a C-130 with U.S. Army Rangers to resupply troops training in Northern California.

On January 12, 2009 I was invited to the Oval Office in the White House to meet with President George W. Bush for work I did with the Department of Defense.

I taught several courses in Durban and Johannesburg, South Africa. It's a beautiful country, with a lot of good people there, but a lot of crime and political turmoil.

I (on the right) am with a few of my operators and armored vehicles, as the Team Leader of the Special Response Team; the equivalent of a civilian S.W.A.T. team.

As shown here in my Women's Survival course in Solingen, Germany I introduced safety gear (helmets, elbow & knee pads, eye protection) for training to Europe.

My Terrorism Survival course, created in 2003, was the first course in the world to teach civilians how to survive terrorist and active shooter attacks. This is in Italy.

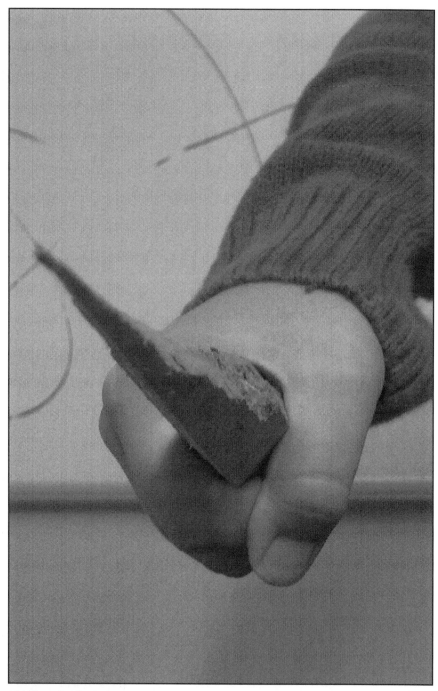

This is a photo of a 10-year-old boy holding a broken piece of wood in a classroom. Such an improvised edged weapon must be treated in the same manner as a knife, because it is just as lethal if the point penetrates your body.

Day 1

A piece of wood can kill you

Too many martial arts schools train with only rubber, plastic, or blunt metal knives to learn self-defense against knife attacks. Do you?

Obviously, learning how to defend against knives is a mandatory requirement, especially since knives are one of the most widely used weapons in the world by criminals and terrorists. But training only with training tools that look like knives conditions your brain for that particular edged weapon. As such, when someone has a sharp piece of wood in their hand, in a real situation that is, your brain may not immediately associate this object as equally dangerous as a metal blade.

To condition your brain to associate all sharp or pointy objects as life threatening, you need to start using a wider variety of training tools. A sharp piece of wood in the hands of a schoolboy is just as deadly as a metal combat knife in the hands of a terrorist. That sharp piece of wood can go through your eyeball, your stomach, or sever one of your arteries just as easily as a metal knife can. In fact, there is a knife maker that I know in Thailand, and all of his edged weapon products are made entirely of hard woods. Law enforcement officers are shocked at just how hard and pointy they are when, on occasion, I have shown them in class.

To simulate a sharp piece of wood (in prison this improvised weapon is known as a "shank") you can tear up a piece of foam to the correct shape of a wooden shank, and then paint it the color of wood. You can use cheap Tempera paint found in most major retail department stores, and certainly in all art or craft shops.

Obviously, with any object you use in contact training, you need the proper eye protection for you and your training partner. When your training partner attacks you with this realistic looking object in his or her hand, your mind, coupled with the proper techniques and tactics, imprints the survival experience into your memory. Therefore, in the event that a real attacker grabs a sharp piece of wood, and comes at you in a threatening manner, your mind retrieves this past training experience, relays the information to you that the object is life threatening, and the result is that your reaction time is reduced, and your decision abilities are more accurate. Through repetition of techniques and scenarios you develop *muscle memory*; memories stored in your brain based on frequently enacted tasks of your muscles.

Taking it a step further, you should not just train for sharp pieces of wood, but anything that can be used as an edged weapon. I like to go into toy stores and buy toys that look like real tools: screwdrivers, hammers, pliers, etc. The plastic toy tools can be painted, and then scratched up, in order for them to look like real metal tools. That realistic screwdriver coming at you may not be a real weapon, but it is a real experience.

As a professional self-defense instructor I'm always using various edged weapons training tools when teaching my Knife Survival courses. If I have learned one thing traveling around the world it's that criminals use a wide variety of edged weapons. Whenever I train a police department, jail, or prison, they usually show me some of the latest weapons they confiscated from the bad guys (either the actual item or a photograph of it).

When I am in museums I am always documenting the weapons that I come across, both ancient and modern, for my ongoing human conflict research. To the right are two photos I took for that research. I've included them to give you more ideas. So, after making a wooden shank replica out of foam, you can then make a bone knife replica out of foam for another training session. If you want a good example of just how deadly a sharpened bone can be then watch the *t bone neck stab* scene performed by actor Gerard Butler in the movie *Law Abiding Citizen* (2009).

Training for a violent world.

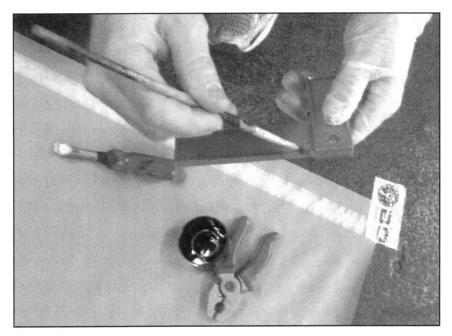

One of my students applies touches of black Tempera paint to these plastic toys to make them look like real used metal tools. The next step is to scratch up the paint.

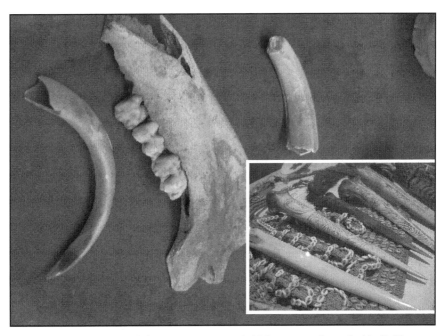

A couple of photos I took in two museums. A 13th-century bone knife (left) excavated near a German castle, and some bone knives from the South Pacific.

These are my fellow recruits on the shotgun range at the police academy in 1991. The only thing we were allowed to have in our primary hand, also known as the "weapon hand," when not in the classroom, was a non-lethal or lethal weapon.

Day 2

Always keep your primary hand free

As a martial artist you should never have any object in your primary hand whenever you are standing or walking in a potentially hostile environment. So, what is your "primary hand?"

Your primary hand, also referred to as the "weapon hand" by professionals, is determined by your handedness. If you are right-handed then that is your primary hand. If you are left-handed, which is about 10% of the population is, the left is your primary hand. Approximately 1% of the population on earth is ambidextrous, meaning they feel equally comfortable using the same weapon in either hand.

Unfortunately, some self-defense instructors refer to the primary hand as the "strong hand," but I don't. I refuse to. Words are powerful, and if you think of your dominant hand as "strong," then that must mean that the other one is "weak." I don't have a weak hand. Just as I don't have a "strong weapon" and a "weak weapon" when serving on my security team. Although my assault rifle is more powerful than my pistol, the rifle is deployed if I need to hit the attacker from a greater distance than the pistol was designed for, or I need more stopping power for certain tactical situations. However, if I had to search some small rooms or closets in a building I'd rather rely on my pistol, because it is easier to use in confined spaces. Granted, the pistol has less stopping power than the rifle, but it is just as lethal. Likewise, my primary hand has one purpose, and my secondary hand has another.

The primary hand must always remain free to deploy your weapon or to grab or push the person you are protecting. Of course, depending on your "reality," a weapon can mean a manufactured weapon, such as a gun or a knife, or an improvised weapon: tactical pen, tactical flashlight (torch), or a common object allowed by law.

When I was a recruit in the police academy the Tactical Officers, which are equivalent to drill sergeants in the military, warned me and my fellow classmates that we were NEVER to have anything in our primary hand except a weapon: baton, pistol, or long gun (shotgun or assault rifle). Anything else in that hand when standing or walking was strictly forbidden. To make sure that we never forgot this cardinal rule the Tactical Officers would scream to the top of their lungs at the violator who was caught, "What is in your weapon hand? Is that a notebook in your hand?" These guys could spot a violator from clear across the campus. Second, came severe punishment. It was usually in the form of a lot of push-ups on the spot followed by a direct order to complete a formal hand-written report that was due the next morning. In this two-page report the recruit had to explain their failure to follow directions, and how to remedy it. Obviously, in the classroom we were allowed to have a writing pen in our primary hand or a field dressing if we were doing first aid training. The rule of keeping the primary hand free only applied to tactical situations.

The purpose of the "harassment" was so that we recruits would never have anything in our primary hand, while out in the field, in order to do a quick draw of the pistol or deploy the long gun during an ambush.

It did not take too many weeks in the police academy until I, like a Pavlov experiment dog, experienced instant fear if I had anything in my primary hand, other than a weapon, when I was standing or walking in this setting. So relentless was the enforcement of this survival rule that to this very day, three decades after I graduated, I don't feel comfortable with anything in my right hand (for I am right-handed), except a weapon, when I am in public. Starting today you need to keep your weapon hand free when out in public, or in a potentially hostile environment, when you are standing or walking. Even if you may not have a firearm on you, as a law enforcement officer or soldier would have, you still must have some sort of "weapon" on you, within reach of your primary hand, and be able to get to it without delay. You must always think tactically.

Training for a violent world.

That's me a few years after the police academy when I was a police bicycle patrol officer. I always keep my primary hand free for my weapon when out in the field.

A dead animal (inset photo) points to the location where I found it on the side of the road while I was patrolling the U.S.-Mexican border during a joint military-U.S. Border Patrol operation on July 30, 2010 when I was a Military Police soldier.

Day 3

Dead animal? Or is it a deadly weapon?

Take a good look at the photos to the left that I took. The inset photo is that of a dead animal on the side of an access road along the United States-Mexican border in California when I was part of a joint military and U.S. Border Patrol operation several years ago. I found the decomposing carcass on the side of the road in the bushes where federal agents patrol in order to prevent people from illegally entering the country. Now, the question to you is, "Is it just a dead animal or is it an Improvised Explosive Device (IED) stuffed into the carcass of a dead animal?"

What would you do if you found a dead animal along side a road? Depending upon where you live, probably nothing. To most people it would simply be "road kill" to be ignored. At most someone might call his or her local Animal Control to have it scooped up and disposed of. However, find the same dead animal near a major sporting event, a synagogue or church, a government building, a school, and it may be a terrorist attack just waiting to happen.

When I was a Military Police soldier, stationed at Joint Forces Training Base in Los Alamitos, California, I was tasked as a training NCO (Noncommissioned Officer - a fancy term for "sergeant") when I was not out doing MP missions. A course that I tought to soldiers going to Afghanistan, Iraq, and Kosovo was how to detect, and avoid, IEDs.

In the M.O.U.T. (Military Operations Urban Terrain) facility, which looked like a real city (containing about 50 buildings, dirt and paved roads, street signs, playground, et cetera) I would place various IEDs where I knew the military convoy would have to pass through. Because of my training and experience I knew many of the tricks of the enemies that we were fighting at this time in history (2006 to 2016). One of those tricks was to put an explosive wrapped with shrapnel into a dead animal, arrange it so that it looked natural on the side of the road, and hide the detonation wire leading to it by burying it under some dirt. The insurgent or terrorist, at a safe distance, would wait for the convoy to be within striking distance, thinking that it was only a dead animal on the side of the road, and then BOOM! there would be several "injured and dead"

American soldiers.

Anyway, I never used real dead animals when I was training soldiers at the M.O.U.T. site, although I would have liked to, and so I took realistic looking stuffed animals I bought at the toy store, and then I placed the inert IED into them.

My trick worked every time. Of course, after the scenario was over I would point out the IEDs that my students did not find. They always missed the "dead animal." However, after the training my students never looked at "road kill" quite the same way ever again, especially when they were deployed.

As a civilian I'm still teaching people about dead animal IEDs. I am an armed plain-clothes security officer at my church, and I'm also the chief trainer for our team. Since churches have been bombed in America in the past I make sure that my team knows all about bomb searches, and that includes checking out dead animals if they find any on the property or the road leading up to the property. I also teach other churches to do the same, along with private security companies around the world. Now, I'm not saying you have to dissect the dead animal you may come across one day to see if someone had stuffed a bomb inside it, because you should never touch any suspected explosive device, but should you ever find a dead animal near a potential target you need to investigate it visually. Does it have any wires going into it? Are there indications that it has been cut open? Is it a fresh carcass or is it in a state of decay? If it's just an animal that died there, then call Animal Control for them to come get it. Alternatively, if it's suspicious call the police immediately, but from a distance. A cell phone can activate a bomb due to the radio waves it sends out.

For you self-defense instructors let me give you a word of warning. Whenever I plant training IEDs I make sure that they are well supervised. I don't want a stranger walking into my training area and poking around my IED. I certainly don't want a real police response because someone thought it was the real thing. At the end of the training I also go through my checklist to make sure all of the IEDs are accounted for, and back in the storage box.

In case you were wondering about the animal in the photo on the border, it was only a dead animal. It had no IED in it, and that's why I was able to take the photo. Had it contained an IED I would have turned off all electrical devices, which would have included my phone since signals emitting from a cell phone can possibly activate a bomb.

Training for a violent world.

An observer in the scout vehicle of a military convoy looks for any telltale signs of an IED on the side of the road, or buried under the road, with binoculars.

When a suspicious object is spotted the convoy stops to investigate. If a device is located an alternate route is taken or EOD (Explosive Ordnance Disposal) is called.

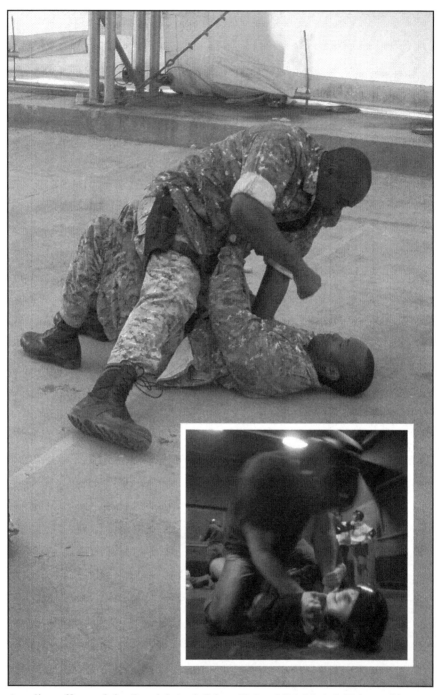

A police officer of the Special Anti-Crime Unit of Trinidad & Tobago (the one being punched) learns why he may have to use deadly force in this position to survive, as does this German woman being choked in my Women's Survival course.

Day 4

Can you kill someone who is on top of you?

Imagine that an unarmed person has mounted you. He is sitting on your stomach as you lay flat on your back, and he is slugging away at your swelling face. What type of force should you use to defend yourself? Reasonable force or deadly force? Should you counterattack by striking back with your fists in the event you can't get the attacker off of you, or should you do an eye gouge or snap his neck? With all things being equal I believe deadly force is justifiable, and I'll explain why from both a tactical and a legal standpoint.

An attacker who is striking downward at you, and who is obviously trying to injure you, has more force as a result of momentum than you have striking upward. The attacker has the force of gravity in his favor, and he can lean into, or drop down, into his strikes. You, on the other hand, are fighting gravity, and your ability to generate forward momentum to increase the power of your strikes is next to nil.

If, while you are on your back, you strike upward at the suspect's face, he can always lean back away from your punches. When you are flat on your back there is absolutely no escape. There is no opportunity of stepping back, and thus you will get the full impact of any descending strike. Even if you manage to make contact with the suspect's face, his head has room to snap backward, and the neck can dissipate the impact force. Not so if you are on the ground getting pummeled. The ground behind your head will either keep your head in a relatively fixed position forcing the head to take 100% of the impact of the blows, or if you do manage to lift your head up slightly the strike to your face will force the back of your head to strike the ground. This is known as secondary impact. Not only do you receive injury from the attacker's fists, but you also receive injury to the head when it impacts the ground. How many times does your head need to bounce off of the ground to cause permanent brain damage? It could be one time, two times, or three. The law states that you do not have to sustain any serious bodily injury. One impact on the ground can knock you out.

The situation I just described to you is justification for the use deadly force (also known as lethal force) against an attacker who is on top of you slugging away at your face, provided you fear for your life and were merely trying to stop the attack. Keep in mind that deadly force does not mean that you have to kill someone or seriously hurt them, but it is an option if no other means are available, such as escaping or using lesser force to stop the aggression.

If you must use deadly force in such a ground fight then punching back like many martial arts systems teach using sport-based techniques, is an uneven trade-off. If someone is using deadly force against you, you had better use deadly force against him or her lest you don't survive. Deadly force options under this circumstance include eye gouges, strikes to the neck, use of weapons, et cetera. That said, deadly force techniques are not going to be natural to you, nor automatic, unless you are in the habit of training using deadly force techniques. Remember, in a real fight you will fall back on your training.

In my Ground Survival courses I'll have the trainer (wearing wrap-around eye protection, a mouth piece, and 12 OZ. boxing gloves) pound on the trainee who is underneath him on a safety mat (wearing only a mouth piece). Contact is moderate (approximately 50% force) for training. The trainee will block one or two of the incoming strikes delivered by the trainer, but instead of trying to punch the trainer back, which we have already determined to be an unequal exchange of force, the trainee will grab onto the trainer (be it hair, an arm, or clothing), and pull him down in order to have the proper distance to apply a deadly force technique to the intended target. The trainer can absorb punches, but is certain to turn away from the trainee who is going for his eyes or neck. The trainer pulling away is good. If the trainer does not pull away, as his human instincts dictate, he will immediately be "disabled" (simulated of course). Either way the trainee can take advantage of the trainer's reaction, and then roll or hip buck the trainer off. Once the attacker is off balance the trainee launches a counter attack or escapes.

Training for a violent world.

This is my Ground Survival logo. It shows the exact situation I described in the article, that being someone on top of you (mounted) pounding on your face.

Instead of someone punching you, you can change the training to where the attacker is stabbing you in the face, neck, and chest, and you must survive the situation.

In the top photo a Brazilian Special Operations police officer does a perfect Pie the Corner technique using an Airsoft training pistol. Below is a French student pretending she has a firearm in her hand in order to better understand the technique.

Day 5

Always Pie the Corner

To "Pie the Corner" is a tactical term which means that before going around a corner where you think there could be a person on the other side waiting to ambush you, you start looking for indications of an ambush one "slice" at a time before going around it.

As you approach the corner of a building you approach it as wide as possible, which will give you more reaction time, and start looking for the tip of a shoe, the edge of a shoulder, or the tip of a weapon before the ambusher sees you first. Remember that the center of his eye is a minimum of 9 inches (23 centimeters) from the edge of his shoulder, and he is probably unaware of just how much of him is exposed before he sees you with that eye closest to the corner. Depending on the situation and environment you can Pie the Corner slow or fast.

For years I had trained thousands of police officers, S.W.A.T. operators, and military personnel how to Pie the Corner tactically with weapons (assault rifles, submachine guns, and pistols). I did it for real thousands of times in my law enforcement and military career. I then took this training and experience and became the first civilian self-defense instructor to teach it to martial artists in my Crime Survival and Terrorism Survival courses, and of course without the weapons (unless you call a mirror or a camera phone a weapon, for I also teach using these two tools to look around a corner in Hot and Warm Zones).

Whenever you are going around any potentially hostile corner you should always take it wide and "pie it" for reasons other than an ambush. A kid on a bicycle could be coming your way at full speed and he or she runs into you. In your own place of business, or in public, it can be someone walking fast and you run into him or her if you don't Pie the Corner. These two techniques will always make things safer for you.

Continuing on, if you do see someone around the corner before they see you, you just bought yourself additional reaction time. Your reaction can be doing a 180-degree turn and escaping from the direction in which you came, or if it was at the last second that you spotted the attacker at least you can take a defensive position when the attacker strikes. In other words, you're not caught totally off guard as you round the corner. Obviously, you should not have headphones in your ears or be on your phone when turning corners, or else you will be distracted and not focused on dangers that may be awaiting you.

You should always Pie the Corner every time you come to an interior or exterior corner, and not just in dangerous neighborhoods or at night. If you make this technique a habit, a part of your daily routine that is, then you will always do it, and thus always be prepared for what may be around the corner.

Training for a violent world.

Two of my Military Police students of the German Army are coming to the corner of the building, and the soldier on the right begins to Pie the Corner.

44

I am showing my Women's Survival students in California how most people walk past a corner, which is eyes straight ahead and no consideration of a possible attack.

My student does the Pie the Corner technique perfectly in Solingen, Germany. As she makes a wide turn she spots the man waiting behind the wall and avoids him.

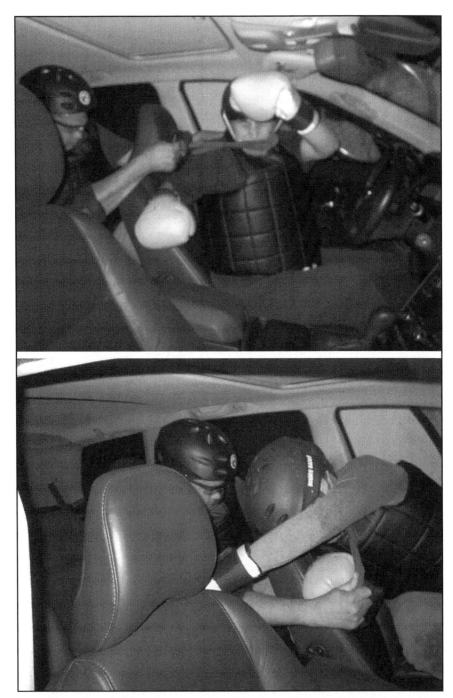

In these two photos an instructor, playing the role of an attacker, tries to strangle (using very light contact) the female students in the front seat of a car. Protective gear, such as helmets, is used to protect the head while doing the techniques.

Day 6

Back seat attack

You should always check the back seat of your car before getting into it in order to make sure that nobody is hiding back there. However, what if you had something on your mind, or you were distracted, and you didn't do your usual visual security scan of the back seat for a possible criminal before getting in? Then, before you start the engine, suddenly a wire gets rapped around your neck tightly, and within three to five seconds you're going unconscious. What are you going to do to survive?

Unless you are well trained in garrote (a length of wire or cord to kill someone by strangulation) defense you're going to waste a couple precious seconds pulling at the wire to get the air and blood circulation that you need, and then when realize you can't get any slack in it you're going to panic. The wasted time does not afford you any more time to try to figure out something new. By then it's too late. I know, because I have placed many of my students into this position in real cars, and I have also simulated this in movie theaters, on city buses, and other seated situations. It's part of my self-defense system called Seat Defense.

The reason that a garrote attack is so difficult to defense against is because the criminal who has placed the weapon around your neck from behind has the advantage, and he can use the back of the seat as leverage by placing a knee or foot in the back of the seat to increase rearward pressure.

Here's the rule that I came up with years ago that is going to save your life. It's the same rule I tell my students in my Improvised Weapons course. It's a Jump Start Command actually that you say to yourself in your mind should this attack occur, and that is, *If the bad guy is behind you, get behind him.*

The only thing that is going to save you is to go with the pull, the direction of the force, get your heels up on the edge of your seat as fast as you can, hurl yourself over the seat, and get into the back seat with the bad guy. First, he is not expecting this bold move, and second, as you rotate over the top of the back support portion of the seat you are rotating the wire or cord around to the back of your neck, which is a lot easier to deal with.

Now, if you think there is no space to do this technique I can tell you now that I've had many students clear that narrow space between the top of the seats and the ceiling of the car. It's awkward, but doable in most vehicles. Plus, when you do this technique it will be with what the United States Marines call "Violence of Action," meaning that you are going to give it 100% as violently and as determined as you can, because you get only one opportunity to do it. Once you are in the back seat with the criminal you then need to be the "wet cat." In other words, go crazy on him, and use whatever technique you can to stop him. Remember, he just placed a garrote around your neck, which is an act of trying to take your life, and so any legal expert would agree that deadly force is warranted.

This same rule, *If the bad guy is behind you, get behind him* also applies to when you are standing and someone comes up behind you to choke you with their arm around your neck or they place a garrote there. If they have a garrote around your neck while you are standing then turn immediately and face the attacker. Attack the attacker! If it is a choke hold with his arm then you drop your center of gravity while pulling the choking arm downward, step behind the attacker, which is easy to do, and with your free hand behind his back pull on his shoulder to the rear and sit down while pulling and leaning back. This will bring the attacker down to the ground, and he will probably smash the back of his head on the ground behind him. However, this technique is for another lesson found in my Control & Defense course.

There is only one way to see if this technique will work inside of a car or not, and that is to go try it in a real car; preferably one you don't mind getting scuffed up. If you do have a nice car, then just go through the motions very slowly with your partner wearing socks on your feet. By practicing a few times you'll reduce the reaction time in a real attack.

Training for a violent world.

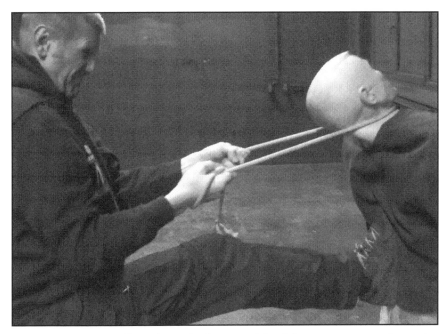

This Swiss security officer does "the Sun Tzu thing," *know your enemy*, by applying a garrote to a mannequin. This in turn leads to knowing the defensive moves.

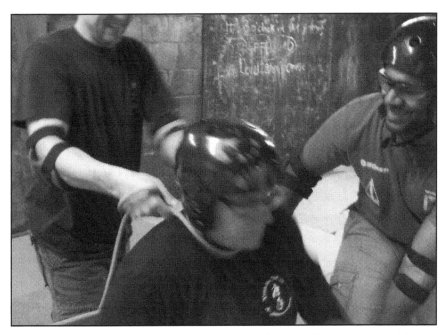

In my self-defense school one instructor plays the role of the attacker while the other holds the bench steady to simulate a garrote attack on a bus, train, or theater.

That's me in the above photo, the Noncommissioned Officer in Charge of Security Forces (SECFOR), protecting the ultimate military drone - the MQ-1 Predator. It is armed with two Hellfire missiles. Then, when I was in a national park in Italy, I took this photo of a sign at the entrance of the park that states OFFENDERS WILL BE REPORTED AND PUNISHED ACCORDING TO CURRENT LAWS.

Day 7

Are drones a security threat to you?

An Unmanned Aerial Vehicle (UAV), commonly known as a drone, is an aircraft without a human pilot aboard that is usually controlled in real-time by remote control by an operator. The most popular type of drone today for civilians is a quadcopter, which is easily recognizable with its horizontal rotor systems mounted on top of the vehicle at the four corners. Many of them look just like toys, and some of them are just that. However, many off-the-shelf drones may be used for nefarious purposes; like carrying explosives and destroying people and property on the ground; an idea that began with militaries around the world using fixed-wing drones to strike military value targets or stop terrorists dead in their tracks.

More and more terrorists, and even criminals, are using drones to commit their evil acts, and that's because drones are affordable and easy to fly. Most are equipped with a high-resolution video camera, and the really good ones, the ones that have internal gyroscopes for stabilization, can hover perfectly still for long periods of time. Drones are fairly quiet, a loud humming noise at most, and you might not even hear it moving through the air space above you with other ambient noise around. So, what does this have to do with you and self-defense? For one thing, an "enemy" can send a drone over your property, hover it in front of a window, and start capturing live-feed video of your activities. Then that same enemy can post it all over YouTube for the world to see. In other words, your privacy can be easily invaded.

You might be saying, "I've got nothing to hide. So what?" But, with drones it can get worse. If a drone can carry a camera, and in some cases large heavy cameras for Hollywood movies, then a drone can also carry a firearm, a hand grenade, or a deadly chemical weapon payload that can be activated with the push of a remote-control button. An even cheaper method to do somebody harm is to have a micro drone, one that can fit in the palm of a hand, armed with a syringe mounted to the front of it. Flying at high speed it flies right into its human target, like a Kamikaze, shoving the needle into the flesh. Upon contact, a sensor has a small piston push the bleach, acid, or rat poison into the puncture wound instantaneously. Have three or four of these things coming at you at once, and you're in some serious danger. If you are the target of the criminal or terrorist, then a drone is a simple way to get to you without the attacker actually being there in the Kill Zone.

If things are set up right the drone operator can actually be in a different country when the attack goes down. The technology is already available. A drone can be staged (such as on a nearby rooftop until the time it is needed), the operator hops onto a flight to another country, and then calls the drone (cell phone activated) to turn it on, and then controls its flight path using just a phone using an app. Since the drone is equipped with a video camera, sometimes multiple cameras looking in different directions, the operator can see exactly where the drone is going, and then release, fire, or inject its deadly cargo when the target is line of sight.

Amazon caused quite a stir in 2013 when it announced that it would be delivering small packages using drones. A lot of people thought it was a publicity gimmick, but it made the United States government examine the possibility. For the first time the commercial use of drones had to be seriously considered. Questions swirled about like, "Would they be allowed to fly over buildings?" "Would they have to follow streets and freeways?" "What if one crashes?" As a result the United States Federal Aviation Administration implemented Unmanned Aircraft Systems rules, testing, and certification. Unfortunately, terrorists and criminals are notorious for ignoring laws.

The wake up call came on February 2, 2015 when a small drone (a DJI Phantom, which was the most popular drone on the market tht year) crashed on the White House grounds. It turned out that the drone was owned and operated by a federal worker who meant no harm, but for the U.S. Secret Service it raised serious questions about the aerial defense of the White House. The drone was too small and too slow to be detected by radar. Yes, there are radars that do pick up small devices, but they can easily be confused with birds by the radar operator.

Although most drones fly by radio signals (transmitted from a phone or remote control device), a drone can be preprogrammed to fly to its destination without radio uplinks or downlinks. Therefore, jamming signals may not always work to stop an incoming killer drone.

If you do see a drone flying about your property or place of work you need to determine the operator's intent. For example, if the drone was hovering over your swimming pool while you were swimming, or hovering outside of a window (day or night), then it is most likely a "peeping drone." That is a crime and a police report needs to be taken. You do not know where those video images will end up.

A drone may not only be used to "spy" on you while at home, but it may be used for surveillance. Someone from an undetected safe distance can fly the drone high above your car and follow you. Your "reality" determines your target value. If you are a high value target (a politician, a celebrity, a Fortune 500 CEO, a law enforcement officer out in the field, et cetera) then it would not be a bad idea to look up once in a while when you are driving or out in the open on foot. Always think spherical when it come to security.

Unfortunately, there is no easy way to disable an incoming drone short of having high-tech equipment always on hand: net or string-carrying anti-drone drones to entangle the killer drone rotors, radio frequency jamming devices (anti-drone jammers), trained birds of prey (also known as anti-drone birds), and drone-blinding lasers to interfere with a drone's guidance camera. Shooting down a drone with a firearm is not wise, for what goes up (a bullet or projectile) must come down. First of all you'd have to be one crack shot if it were diving at you, and second, discharging a firearm into the air is illegal in most jurisdictions; not to mention that *what goes up must come down* (the bullet or slugs). Therefore, the best way to get away from a drone is to get behind cover (a large object that can stop projectiles, explosives, or gas) preferably inside of a building with the door closed behind you. It's like trying to get away from a bullet, only worse. A drone can follow you.

Now that you've had a chance to think about it, it is quite clear that dealing with weaponized drones will be one of the greatest self-defense challenges for many years to come.

Training for a violent world.

Flying bottles or rocks are no respecter of persons, and this is why these two female students are practicing my original technique Flexible Shield Against Thrown Projectiles Evacuation. In this case the "flexible shield" used is a cable-knit sweater.

Day 8

Flexible Shield Against Thrown Projectiles Evacuation

It's Happy Hour and you are snacking on some tasty treats and washing it down with a cold drink with a person you care about at the table. Suddenly the place erupts into a destructive fight, and soon bottles and glasses start to fly about the room. Any one of these projectiles could cause serious injury to you, or the person you are protecting (called the *principal* in bodyguard jargon), if they strike the head. So, how do you get yourself, and the principal, out of the impact zone and to the exit without getting nailed by a projectile? It just so happens that several years ago I created a self-defense technique to address this very scenario. It's the Flexible Shield Against Thrown Projectiles Evacuation.

A "flexible shield" is nothing more than a jacket, a sweater, pullover, a tablecloth, or even a towel. Once projectiles start flying, you need to get that flexible shield up just above the top of your head and stretch it tight with the FRONT TOWARD ENEMY. In essence you are creating a net that will stop the airborne object upon contact, causing it to either bounce off the flexible shield or fall straight to the floor once it loses energy. You'll be behind it of course, and your principal will be behind you, as you both make your way to the door, and to safety. Yes, you may get a finger or two hit on the way, but it's better than vital targets getting struck.

When I train my students how to survive this type of attack I have the "attacker" throw boxing gloves (light contact only) at the escaping students. Since objects are being thrown at people's heads I have the bodyguard and the principal wear the minimum protective equipment of eye protection. After all, even a boxing glove can scratch the eyeball if it hits at the right angle. If the objects being thrown are a little harder, such as tennis balls, which are the training projectiles I like to use when I train police and military riot units, I'll have the "victims" equipped with skateboard helmets. Remember, safety first.

One time, while I was teaching a course called Bar Fight Survival, in an actual bar located in a small town called Waldbrunn in the Black Forest of Germany, I took my students outside to the parking lot and I threw real glass beer bottles at them as they performed the technique. Of course, I was extremely careful in keeping the velocity of the trajectories as slow as possible, and my aim was at head and chest level. At first, each two-person team was a bit frightened, but once they felt the bottles bouncing off of the flexible shield as they move out of the impact zone their confidence was gained having experienced "the real thing." Now, if you don't feel confident with real glass bottles you can always use emptied plastic soft drink bottles. They look like the real thing, but they are lighter and won't break when they hit the ground. Oh yes! When we finished this training in Waldbrunn there was a big mess of broken glass to be cleaned up.

As you know, there are only 10 directions in this universe: forward, back, right, left, up, down, and the letter "X" (four diagonal directions). As such, when you practice my Flexible Shield Against Thrown Projectiles Evacuation technique you can't just practice it going in one direction to get away from the projectiles. You have to learn to hold the flexible shield up while going right, left, retreating, or even going diagonally, because you never know what direction you'll have to go in a real situation.

Unless you are on a riot squad this situation is a rare occurrence, and as such you need to practice the technique only once or twice a year.

Training for a violent world.

Empty plastic bottles, used as projectiles, are good training props. Also, doing the training in a realistic environment is far superior than doing it in a training hall.

The "flexible shield" idea came to me having trained thousands of police and military personnel, like my students here with the Los Angeles Sheriff's Department.

I love my nephew Gary. He's a little warrior. Not only has he trained in the same Mixed Martial Arts gym as Ronda Rousey, but he has studied Judo, winning many trophies and medals in competitions all over California. He also studies under me.

Day 9

Dirty Tricks

My 12-year-old nephew Gary participated in a Judo tournament. He has won many matches in the past, but this time he lost both of his matches that eliminated him from the competition.

Over the years I've encouraged Gary, along with his father Greg who is my brother-in-law, to compete in both Judo and Karate tournaments on a regular basis. In addition to his sport-based and traditional-based training, I've been teaching him my Reality-Based Personal Protection system ever since he first started learning how to walk.

Using this teachable moment at his Judo tournament I said to Gary, as he was cooling down and feeling the bitterness of defeat, "It was a good thing that these were not life and death fights."

He responded confidently, "Uncle Jim, if my two fights had been life and death fights I would have used dirty tricks to win."

I was proud of his answer, and I said to him, "Good answer. You're right."

For years I have been teaching Gary the legal issues concerning the use-of-force when it comes to self-defense, and he knows the difference between controlling force, reasonable force, and deadly force. Thus, his answer was perfect. It's a lot better than what most martial artists would answered, and that is, "Better to be judged by twelve than carried by six."

Gary knows that in a schoolyard fistfight he is limited to using controlling force or reasonable force against a big bully, but had this day been a life and death fight, instead of a Judo competition, he'd have the option of using deadly force. To survive the ordeal, if escape were not possible, he would have most likely resorted to an eye gouge, crushing the attacker's throat, biting, or using a weapon - even if it were a pencil. Finally, he'd know the justification for the amount of force applied, the right words to say to the police, and he'd be ready to appear in court.

We can all learn a little something from Gary's comment to me.

Training for a violent world.

A Security Forces (SECFOR) soldier under my command investigates a possible burglary. She uses the technique that I taught her to see if any contact was made with the glass of the window. The only tool needed to do this is a flashlight (torch).

Day 10

Checking for a burglar

Most house burglaries happen in the daytime, because most burglars know that the residents will be at work or out doing errands. On the other hand, most commercial burglaries are done at night when the business is closed, and no employees are expected to be there.

From my experience of many years as a patrol police officer south of Los Angeles, a deputy sheriff Field Supervisor, and a Military Police (MP) sergeant patrolling a base, I know that most burglars breaking into homes or business do so when nobody is in there to avoid a confrontation. Approximately 70% of all crime is drug related, and most burglars just want to get in, take something of value, get out, go pawn the merchandise, go buy their drugs, and then purchase what they need and want after that (food, a motel room, sex, or whatever). However, there are a small percentage of burglars who break into people's homes at night, and these criminals are known as "cat burglars." It sounds like a cute title, but it's anything but cute. This type of burglar is extremely dangerous, because they know that there is a likelihood of a physical confrontation with the residents, and they are prepared for it. This is why punishment by the courts is more severe for cat burglars.

If you're coming home at night, or you have to go into a closed business where you work, and you are on the exterior about to unlock the door and go inside, don't do it if you see evidence that someone may have entered illegally. Get to a safe distance and call the police. It's the job of the police to search the premises if you suspect a burglar is inside the building.

The obvious signs of a break in are: a door is ajar, there are pry marks on the door and the door frame, a window is open or broken, you see a beam of light from a flashlight (a "torch" for you in the Common Wealth) moving about, or there are items that look as if they had been dropped near the entrance. However, there can also be signs of a burglary that are not so obvious, and untrained people would miss them completely. One police technique that I learned from my Field Training Officer (FTO), back when I was a rookie at the Costa Mesa Police Department in 1991, was the Flashlight Against the Window.

Many burglars make entry into houses or businesses through windows. Often burglars don't have to break the glass to get in because people sometimes forget to lock windows. All the burglar has to do is put his hands on the window, apply a little pressure, and slide the window open. Once he crawls inside the building he slides the window back in place so nobody from the outside would notice the illegal penetration.

The way you see if someone has tampered with a window is to come up to the window, place your flashlight directly on or slightly away from the glass, and shine it along the surface of the glass. Think of your flashlight as lying on the glass while turned on even though it is a vertical plane. The dust that is clinging to the glass shows up quite well at this angle, like trees casting long shadows from the setting sun, and if someone had placed their fingers or the palm of their hand on the glass you will see that the dust has been disturbed, because where the fingers or hands had touched the dust is missing from the contact points. In other words, there is a clean area. You would never see this disturbance unless you shine the light sideways to the glass. The darker the environment, the clearer the image will be. Unless the window was washed that day, there will always be a film of dust on the window. The more time between window washings the more dust film will be attached to it. You've seen the back windshield of a dirty car where some adolescent wrote into the dust, WASH ME. The Flashlight Against the Window technique is not quite that visible, but it's still there.

If you do see signs that someone recently touched the window, you do not want to touch it. If the burglar did not wear gloves there may be forensic evidence on the glass, namely latent fingerprints or a palm print. This may be the only evidence to identify the criminal.

The Flashlight Against the Window is a technique you can easily master. Tonight, go outside and touch an exterior window with your hand. Then take your flashlight and try the technique as I described. Once you have the technique mastered have someone you know go touch another window without you looking, as if they had been trying to slide it open like a burglar would, and then examine the window to see if you find proof of the "break in." This way you are putting the technique into the context of a scenario.

Training for a violent world.

Evidence of someone's finger having touched this dusty back windshield is apparent by the disruption of the dust (the "clean" area) with the words WASH ME!

Me (left) with the Costa Mesa Police Department in 1997 pulling a graveyard shift, which always included investigating a few burglary calls on a nightly basis.

The instructor on the right is yelling and screaming at the student to induce some stress as he fires upon a photorealistic target. Under stress gross motor skills take over the body. Therefore the aim point must be center mass of the target.

Day 11

Just go for center mass

The public seems to think that a police officer should be able to shoot a gun or knife out of the hand of a criminal in a life-and-death situation. When I was a police officer I responded to a few hostage situations, and after the crisis was over I heard a few naïve citizens ask, "Why didn't you guys just shoot the weapon out of the man's hand?"

Anyone with any gun skills knows that shooting a weapon out of someone's hand in a combat situation is next to impossible, even at close range. It looks good in the movies, which was choreographed and rehearsed many times before the final cut was made, but it's just not going to happen in real life. The target is too small, it's moving, and it's very difficult to hit. If a police officer misses such a shot, and most will, the hostage's life is in jeopardy. In fact, even highly trained S.W.A.T. police officers would also not be comfortable taking such a risky shot.

Most police departments around the world correctly teach their officers to aim for center mass if lethal force is required. The term "center mass," means just that; aiming for the center mass of the target. When the criminal is standing upright that usually means the center of the chest. If the criminal is kneeling down, with his side to the police officer offering a smaller target profile, center mass would then be the lower rib cage. The reason center mass is targeted is because shooting requires a great deal of skill to begin with, and in a fluid combat situation any bullet striking a human silhouette is considered a good shot. Hitting center mass is the goal, but with any movement made by the criminal, or the police officer, the bullet could strike further away from the aim point. Therefore, as much space as possible is needed to keep from missing.

Unfortunately, there are some police departments in the world that require their police to "shoot to wound" with one shot, and then assess the situation before taking another shot. In a life-and-death situation this is an asinine restriction, and one which was made by the politicians who are not grounded in tactical realities. A wounded suspect can still kill.

Throughout my law enforcement, military, and private security career

I have always qualified as EXPERT with my pistol. If someone would have told me back then, or even now, that I had to shoot the weapon out a criminal's or terrorist's hand, I'd tell him or her, "You're crazy!" Perhaps a sniper could pull it off with a long gun, provided the target is within 100 meters with little to no movement, but other than that, forget it! I'm a trained sniper, so I know what I am talking about.

Along the same line, there are many martial arts instructors teaching their students that they can punch precise pressure points on the human head when in a real physical confrontation. Mind you, the attacker is most likely moving, blocking, and trying to tear your head off as well. Instructors who teach such nonsense are just like those people who say the police should shoot the weapon out of a criminal's hand.

You probably have guessed already that I don't instruct my students to strike an exact spot when targeting the head. I don't say, "Go for the tip of the nose!" or "Hit him on the jaw!" like I recall my traditional-based and sport-based instructors telling me. Rather, I teach them to just go for "center mass!" If they aim for the center of the mass, then they are bound to hit somewhere on the head as the fist and fur are flying. Even when I am teaching an eye gouge for deadly force situations, and the eye is a very small target to hit, most students can't succeed with a finger poke in a realistic scenario. What works best is when they place the palm of their hand on the attacker's ear allowing the thumb to slip into the eye socket from there. That, or rake the face with an open hand claw where one finger is bound to go into the eye during the downward motion.

Due to movement, blocking, and an attacker's own self-preservation instincts a lot can go wrong in a real fight, and that's exactly why I stick to sound principles, like striking center mass; be it with a firearm or an empty hand strike.

The best training tool for mastering center mass head strikes are martial arts mitts that are shaped like the human head; complete with eyes, nose, and a mouth. There are a few products on the market, but all of them have some type of handle where the trainer can hold it up for the trainee to strike, much like a focus glove. When the trainer moves, the head moves, and when the trainer retreats the trainee can pursue the target or escape.

If you stick to the center mass principle you'll be a lot more effective, because it simplifies target acquisition in your mind. The result will be reduced reaction time, and more realistic expectations.

Training for a violent world.

The corrections officer on the right lands a solid punch to the face of the S.W.A.T. officer. I taught both of these students, "Just aim for center mass, like in shooting."

Even when doing a head butt, center mass (between the top of the head and above the top lip) is the aim point as this female Dutch police officer is doing here.

This S.W.A.T. team is about to board a school bus where a man has taken a woman hostage. Their prior training and experience will determine if the mission will be a success or not. The same holds true for your next "mission" that you will face.

Day 12

You're only as good as your last mission

When I was a team member on the Costa Mesa Police Department S.W.A.T. team, back in the 1990s, we had an expression, "You are only as good as your last mission." So, what does this mean? It means that if a tactical team had a successful mission at the last call out (activation) then it is a successful S.W.A.T. team. However, if the last mission was a failure, then the team is deficient and in need of better and harder training. It doesn't matter if the three missions before were all successful; a bad mission could become a repeated pattern, and if not properly corrected, citizens and team members could be injured or killed at the next one.

The same holds true for martial artists. I'll substitute the word "mission" with the word "fight." *You are only as good as your last fight.* Perhaps your last fight was an ego fight on the schoolyard umpteen years ago, or for some of you it was a life-and-death fight in Fallujah, Iraq. So, not only are there different types of fights, there are also different types of intensity.

S.W.A.T. teams are used to dealing with the worst violence imaginable, and so they have a good idea of the kinds of situations they'll face at their next mission. The same is true for any professional who fights for a living: military operators, executive protection, bouncers, et cetera. The question for you is, "Are you training for the worst-case scenarios that you may face on your next 'mission?" For many of you reading this, the fight that may be coming in the near or distant future will be your first "mission" ever. Regardless, are you training for a real enemy or someone who uses the same techniques as you, because you are locked in the groupthink mentality? Are you training with a cooperative partner, or are you simulating what the real bad guys would do that you will confront? Are you ready for that sniper picking people off in the street? Are you ready for a poisonous gas being released in a metropolitan area? Are you even aware of how street criminals select their targets? After all, you are only as good as your last mission.

Training for a violent world.

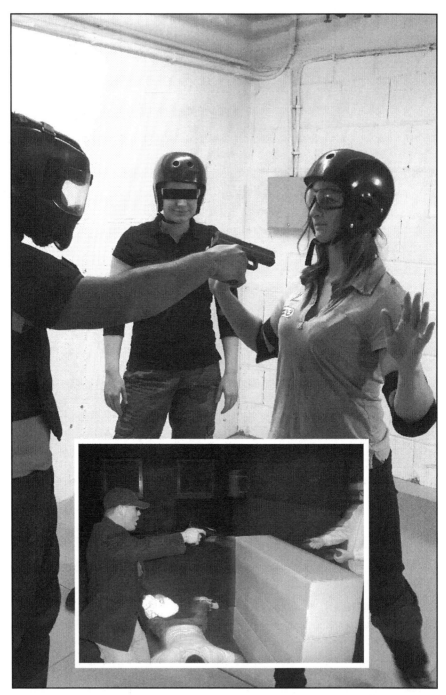

A criminal may get close to a woman, because he doesn't fear her like he does a man, such as in this Women's Survival course (large photo). However, most robberies take place at the distance shown (inset photo) in this Crime Survival scenario.

Day 13

Deception, Distraction, or Distance

Most martial arts instructors, even supposed "reality-based" ones, teach gun disarm techniques when the gun is within reach. However, in the majority of armed robberies, the criminal has his gun out of reach of the victim. This is the distance very few martial arts instructors teach their students about. However, I do in my Crime Survival course. The rule to survival, when it comes to gun disarms, is *If you can touch the gun, you can take the gun. If you can't touch the gun, you can't take the gun.* It's as simple as that. Think about it. What are you going to do if you are out of reach of the gun? Take a suicide leap towards it and risk the crimianl having a sympathetic reflex? Or, you can try running away and risk getting shot in the back. What will help you in this situation is The Three Ds for a gun out of reach: Deception, Distraction, or Distance.

DECEPTION - In order to close the gap, so that you can get closer to the criminal to get within reach of the gun, you use deception. You act like you are complying with the demands to lure the criminal into believing that you are too afraid to resist or fight back, and then once you are close enough to touch the gun you have the opportunity to take the gun.

DISTRACTION - The criminal has asked you to hand over your wallet, but based on the situation you are convinced that he is going to shoot no matter what you do. Therefore, as you are handing the criminal your wallet you suddenly toss it towards his eyes, move off line to avoid a sympathetic response shot, and either attempt a disarm or start running away. If he is distracted by something else, then it's even better for you.

DISTANCE - Distance is always to your advantage when somebody is about to shoot you, or they are shooting at you. The more distance you gain the less accurate the shots will be. Perhaps you can increase the distance by taking a few steps back while getting robbed, or you just go for it and start running. Just one leap and you're already a yard away (1 meter).

Training for a violent world.

An instructor (playing the role of an armed robber) robs a convenience store with an Airsoft pistol in a Crime Survival scenario. During the post-conflict part of the training, the students ("victims") are interviewed by a real off duty police officer.

Day 14

Put some emotion into the police report

In any fight, be it a shoving match or a full-blown terrorist attack, there is pre-conflict, the conflict, and post-conflict. Most self-defense systems teach conflict, the actual fight, but they tend to neglect the other two aspects of combat. However, reality will not ignore the other two. They are going to happen. One result of post-conflict is coming face to face with the police, especially if it was a serious crime. Whenever the police get involved they're going to write a report about the incident you were involved in. It will be documented, and what you tell them is critical.

If you are ever the victim of a crime, you need to let the police officer interviewing you know exactly what you were feeling, your emotions, at the time of the crime. In some crimes fear has to be present in what the law calls the "elements of the crime." For example, the elements for the crime of robbery are *the felonious taking of personal property in the possession of another, from his person or immediate presence, and against his will, accomplished by means of force or fear*. Without force or fear the act becomes merely theft with perhaps a weapons charge if the criminal was armed. If you want justice, meaning putting the attacker behind bars, you must tell the police officer that you had to give him what he wanted (force). Why do people, 9 times out of 10, give the robber what he wants? It's because they are afraid of getting hurt (fear). Remember, the law states "by means of force **or** fear." The word "or" is a key word. There are occasions when fear is not a factor, like if a criminal comes up behind you, knocks you down to the ground, takes your shopping bag (theft), and runs off before you even realized what happened. You were caught completely by surprise, and thus there was no time to be afraid.

A man with a knife or gun in your face is someone to be feared. A robbery is a felony. As such, it is necessary to explain to the police officer what you believed the emotional state of the criminal was, along with your own. Don't just make your official statement, "He pointed a gun at me and demanded my money, and so I gave it to him." Yes, the elements of the crime are in there, but the statement is flat and boring, and it does not actually give the whole story. A law enforcement Watch Commander, and attorneys up the line, will read this report. You don't want anything "lost in translation." If it went something like this, then state it, "The man had a wild look in his eyes. He was sweating profusely and screamed at me in a very threatening manner, 'Give me your f*****g money! Now!' and I gave it to him because I was terrified. I mean terrified! I thought at that moment he was going to shoot me if I didn't do what he demanded. He had his finger on the trigger and shoved the pistol up in my face. I really thought I was going to die!"

You need not be so clinical when giving your report to the police. You need to let them know what was going through your mind, and also the demeanor of the criminal. Hopefully the police officer will write down what you told him or her verbatim in the police report soon after the incident, and not at the end of their shift when they are trying to cut corners to get home. Remember, police are human and they don't always put down everything you want them to in the report. Sometimes the police officer puts his or her own "slant" on the report even though they are supposed to be objective and are to state only the facts. Police officers cannot give their opinion in a criminal police report.

As a field supervisor I have seen many very poorly written police reports over the years. For your sake it is even better if the police officer is recording your statement. Many police officers around the world are now "wired" with either a microphone or a body camera recording you. The video footage is uploaded into a computer. This is good, because the recording can be used in a court of law. Those in the courtroom see what the police officer saw.

Ask the police officer outright, "Is this conversation being recorded?" If it is then you know your statements will be accurately recorded. However, remember that police officers can "lie" to you (in the United States anyway) under certain conditions, and it is perfectly legal (there are some guidelines, but I will not go into that). For that matter, you can also record the conversation with the police yourself, unless you live in a repressive country. However, be careful when recording a conversation with the police because the act of you suddenly pulling out a phone could be misinterpreted as you going for a weapon. In other words, you could get shot or rapped with a baton if you suddenly pull out a phone without letting the police officer know what you are doing. When dealing with the police everything must be communicated, and movements slow.

Before the police even approach you, start recording, and put the phone back into your pocket. If you want it to work correctly for you then you have to also practice this technique from time to time in training; another reason why you should wear the clothes you will fight in – *Train as you fight*. In some of my Jim Wagner Reality-Based Personal courses I actually have my students practice recording an "incident" with their phones. I set up realistic scenarios to accomplish this. This is all part of their post-conflict training.

Not to pat myself on the back, but my students are fortunate because their instructor, me, has had over 20 years experience as a law enforcement officer, and as a Military Police soldier (basically the same job with additional military rules and regulations). Since I work in the private security industry, I keep up with current laws, and because my work takes me to different countries, I learn the laws of those countries concerning use-of-force issues.

If you are not a police officer, then hopefully you will have the opportunity to train with one, and he or she can explain the laws that pertain to the techniques and tactics you are practicing. I always like having local police officers in my courses, because I don't hesitate to get their feedback and perspective on the law concerning a particular technique, tactic, or scenario that I am teaching. After all, knowing the law must be a part of your self-defense training. You need to know certain laws before a fight (pre-conflict), what you can legally do and not do in a fight (conflict), and how to articulate what happened to you during the police interview (post-conflict). Ignoring the law of the land is like ignoring needed first aid after an injurious fight.

Training for a violent world.

These are just a few of the weapons on display on June 16, 2018 that were confiscated from criminals who were arrested by the Tustin Police Department in California. Regardless of how many laws there are, criminals will always have weapons.

Day 15

80% of your training should be about weapons

On August 21, 2015 an Islamic Jihadist terrorist Ayoub El-Khazzani, 25-years-old, tried to murder as many passengers as he could on Thalys train 9364 from Amsterdam to Paris.

He had gone into the restroom with a large backpack on only to emerge several minutes later with an AK-47 assault rifle in his hands (which is an illegal weapon in France, by the way) a pistol, a box cutter, 270 bullets, and a bottle of gasoline. Fortunately, three Americans (two of which were in the military at the time of the incident – HOOAH!), two Frenchmen, and a Brit overcame the terrorist when there was a "pause in conflict" – when his weapon jammed, and he was trying to clear the malfunction.

Clint Eastwood produced and directed a movie about this very terrorist attack called *The 15:17 to Paris* (released in 2018), which every martial artist should see. The roles of the three Americans were played by the actual three men who fought with the terrorist, and so every second of the movie fight scene is authentic.

Long before this incident happened I had always taught my students about the Pause in Conflict phenomena. It's a term I coined describing that moment in a conflict, be it a fist fight or a terrorist attack, when a pause will occur. In a fistfight it may be after a few punches have landed and the aggressor momentarily assesses what damage he has done. In a knife attack it could be the moment between where the bad guy looks left and right for any witnesses, and the next where he tries to stab his victim in the gut. It's a small pause, but a pause nonetheless. During a terrorist attack, that Pause in Conflict can be when the weapon jams, as was the case in the 2015 train attack, or when a terrorist is seeking another target to engage. It could also be when a terrorist is distracted, such as a police car rolls up to the scene, which was the case with the Charlie Hebdo shooting that occurred in Paris seven months earlier than the train attack.

A Pause in Conflict can happen for many reasons. When that pause does present itself, you need to take advantage of it by escaping, seeking cover, or launching a counterattack if you're close enough to do so. The heroes on train 9364 took advantage of their Pause in Conflict, for if they had not done so there would have been a lot of carnage.

There's a second principle that I'd like to teach you. The two terrorists attacks I described to you illustrate the need for you to spend more of your self-defense training time dealing with modern weapons (guns, knives, and impact weapons) than empty hand (unarmed person against and unarmed person) techniques, tactics, and scenarios. As such, my general rule to you is that *80% percent of your training should be weapons oriented, and 20% percent should be hand-to-hand combat.* After all, most criminals use weapons, and all terrorists do.

By contrast, most traditional-based and sport-based martial arts have their training time ratio backwards. About 20% of their training is geared towards weapons (and many schools even regress back to ancient weapons only: tonfa, sai, sword, three-sectional staff, spear, nunchacku, et cetera.), and 80% of it is empty hand training (what I refer to as "the proverbial bar fight"). Of course, some systems, like Judo and MMA, don't deal with weapons at all, nor should they, since they are sports, and not self-defense.

Let me share with you a little history that will shed some light on why I came up with this 80:20 ratio. I mentioned to you before that I had written for Black Belt magazine and Budo magazine, starting in 1999 and 2000, but I didn't state the reason why they wanted me to write for them. Well, here it is.

Both publications took a look at my background as a soldier, corrections officer, police officer, S.W.A.T. officer, diplomatic bodyguard, and martial arts instructor, and they were confident that I'd be the one to introduce realistic training through the pages of their magazines (then later through my books and videos they both published) to the martial arts community. If you take a good look at any martial arts magazine in the world that was printed before 1999, you'll know exactly what I am talking about. Editor Robert Young from Black Belt magazine and Publisher Alfredo Tucci from Budo International, gave me free rein to write articles about topics never before published: defense for drive-by shootings, sniper attacks, grenades, bombs, school shootings, office massacres, and terrorist attacks.

Of course, I was breaking new ground at that time in martial arts history, and many of my critics were outraged, traditional-based martial artists mostly, and some even to the point of mocking me publically. In response to an article I wrote about how to defend against terrorist attacks, one well-known martial arts instructor, his name is not important, sent a letter to Robert Young sarcastically asking, "What's next from Jim Wagner? How to survive a nuclear bomb?" My response to the letter to the editor was my next article titled, *How to survive a nuclear bomb blast or dirty bomb*. And why not? I had gone through Nuclear Biological Chemical (NBC) warfare training with the U.S. Army, Weapons of Mass Destruction (WMD) training with the FBI, and Chemical Biological Radiological Nuclear Explosives (CBRNE) with the Europeans.

I also remember another letter to the editor that lambasted me, "Nobody is going to use an AK-47 to shoot people. Jim Wagner is just trying to scare people so they will take his courses."

Obviously, this letter that was intended to make me look foolish had been written before the Amsterdam to Paris train attack of 2015, followed four months later by one of the worse terrorist attacks in California history known as *The 2015 San Bernardino Attack,* leaving 14 people dead and 22 others seriously injured. On that one a husband and wife team, radical Islamic terrorists, were responsible for that attack. Their target was a Christmas party. I happened to have been 30 miles away from there that day teaching a live-fire counterterrorism course to foreign police officers, and two of my friends were actually across the street from the building that was under attack, and they were forced to go to lockdown.

I'm really glad I never listened to the mocking and jeering, because I knew that it was wise to warn the martial arts community of the impending violence I believed was only going to increase based upon my training, experience, and information I was privy to.

Well, it's been over a decade since these letters to the editor were published, and there have been countless attacks, both criminal and terrorism, around the world where assault rifles and explosives were used against innocent civilians; including against children. No, there has not been a nuclear strike yet, but North Korean dictator Kim Jong Un was certainly threatening one in 2017 and early 2018. Plus, factor in all of the knife and impact weapon attacks that continue to take place on a daily basis around the world, and it's no wonder why I place more emphasis on training to defend against weapons than I do empty hand attacks.

Warrior wisdom dictates that you see the world around you as it is, and train for the those attacks that you are most likely to face. That means 80%-20% in training, and taking advantage of any Pause in Conflict should you be attacked.

Training for a violent world.

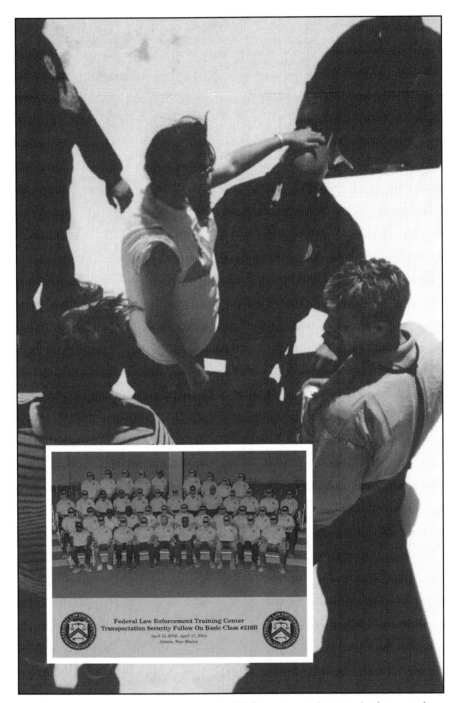

During a counterterrorism scenario at FLETC, a woman (an actor) tries to seduce the federal agent. The agent is armed with not only a firearm, but also a cover story. I am in the center, bottom row (inset photo), with my classmates of Class 216B.

Day 16

Can a "lie" protect you?

Do you have a cover story for strangers who strike up conversation with you if you don't want them to know anything about you? Everyone studying self-defense should have one.

"What's a cover story?" you ask. Well, let me start at the counterterrorism school at the Federal Law Enforcement Training Center (FLETC) in Artesia, New Mexico in 2002. That's where the government sent me after recruited me to help fight the Global War on Terrorism.

In Class 216B, every student was instructed to come up with a "cover story," because we were all going to work undercover in airports and aboard American commercial aircraft around the world as United States Federal Air Marshal agents; "FAM" for short. A cover story is when you tell people you meet while on a mission facts about yourself that are not true, but sound true, so that they will never discover your true identity. One never knows who the enemy may be. The more boring the cover story, the more likely the person trying to engage you in conversation will lose interest in you, and would never guess you to be a government agent.

Even if you're not a government agent going from one country to another waiting to "neutralize" a terrorist, it's a good idea in some situations to conceal your true identity. Having a cover story of your own does this. To come up with a good cover story, you need to change a few facts that are already a part of your own personal history so that you'll easily remember, by heart, the "lies" you intend to use. If someone strikes up a conversation with you, while sitting next to you on public transportation or in a social setting for example, you need to sound convincing. If you are asked what city you live in, you don't give them the actual city you live in, so he or she cannot look you up one day, but you give the name of a different city; one that you have spent a lot of time in. You had better know a lot about that city (street names, restaurants, where the sports stadium is, et cetera), because the person you are talking to may be familiar with that particular city you just named.

Inevitably people will ask you the question, "What do you do for a living?" In my case, back in 2002 when I was in the TERRORIST HUNTING CLUB, I couldn't answer, "I'm a counterterrorist on a mission right now. Don't bother me anymore, because I'm doing surveillance on that suspected terrorist over there." The truth could have obviously compromised the mission. Likewise, for those of you currently with a law enforcement agency or serving a government entity, any information about yourself and your job could compromise local or national security, and in some cases even get you or others killed. So, in order to keep people from probing you for information, and maintain OPSEC, *Operations Security*, you must choose a profession that you are familiar with to create a believable cover story. For example, after college I was in the advertising business for a few years, and so my cover story, if asked, was that I was "an Art Director for an advertising firm." Since I knew all about the profession if someone asked me specific questions, I could answer any questions with authentic details, and they would believe that it was indeed my current profession. I would talk with them for a few minutes, saying that I designed coupons for newspapers, and they would get bored talking with me after a few minutes. However, when you come up with a name of the business that "you work at," you need to have a name and location for your business, because the curious person might ask you for the name of the business and its location. To handle this particular problem with my advertising cover story I would just say, "I'm working freelance now," and give them a bogus phone number and location. "Yeah, give me a call if you ever want some freelance graphics done."

However, a cover story alone is not enough. One must rehearse it (scenario training). When I was in counterterrorism school, the instructor asked all of us, one by one, in the classroom to introduce ourselves using our false names, and speak for a minute or two using our cover stories. The instructors wanted to see if we could convince our classmates, and of course I did. But, I will never forget when the instructor asked the agent sitting behind me, "What do you do for a living?" He replied, "I am a male exotic dancer," and the class busted up laughing. Nobody was expecting a cover story like that. Well, he did have a second cover story, a little more mainstream, but with his muscular physique and handsome looks, he could have very well passed as an exotic dancer.

One day a criminal may be doing surveillance on you. They may seem like a normal person asking you routine questions, but a voice inside of you tells you not to trust them. In this case you may want to have a cover story of your own. You don't want to be talking to a possible terrorist in the lobby of a government building or inside a train going from Amsterdam to Paris, "Yeah, I've been studying martial arts now for fifteen years," because you may be the first person he wants to kill when the guns start coming out. Martial artists tend to brag about their background, because it's the Alpha Dog attitude in them that makes them want to do so, but in most cases it's best to not let people know it.

Several times when I was overseas, an over-curious cab driver asked me, because of my accent, "Are you American?" I unhesitatingly replied, "I'm Canadian, from Vancouver." It throws their scent off, and after all, who hates the Canadians? It's the United States of America, the "Great Satan," many foreign people hate because of indoctrination or jealousy. Just that little statement is a cover story. And, if they start asking me questions about the Vancouver area I can be convincing, because I have taught up there many times, eh.

Is a cover story part of the martial arts? The answer is, "Of course it is." Again, what is the literal term for "martial arts?" You got it, it's "war arts," and there are people out there who are at war with you: crazy people that suddenly snap and go violent because of mental issues, drunks and druggies, criminals, and terrorists. A cover story is just all part of your training to be more reality-based.

Training for a violent world.

A soldier may be required to commit justifiable homicide against enemy combat-ants in warfare. This is one of my Dutch Army students serving in Afghanistan.

When young people play violent video games without proper adult supervision the violence is often taken out of context, and it can lead to unjustified violence.

Day 17

Educating kids to be killers

Not too long ago I was playing the video war game Call of Duty with my 12-year-old nephew Gary. You remember, he's the one in Judo and MMA. He's a good kid, and an honor student.

Anyway, after he "killed" an enemy soldier on the cyber battlefield he moved his avatar, a graphical representation of the user in a virtual world, up to the fallen soldier and started moving the joystick back and forth rapidly. I was confused as to what he was doing because the vibrating movement, which made me slightly dizzy while looking at the big screen, had no combat value. I had played with Gary in the past many times before, and he never did that before. I just had to ask the boy, "What are you doing?"

He didn't hesitate to respond, "I'm humping the body," and told me that he had learned this technique from others.

I was shocked, and sickened, because the English word for "humping" means to have sex. He was "having sex" with the fallen soldier, the act of necrophilia (having sex with a corpse), as a sign of ultimate victory over another human being. I slapped the back of his head lightly to show him my disgust, and I told him, "I don't ever want you doing that again. Do you understand me?"

Gary had learned cyber "humping" from other players online, boys he had never met face to face. Today video games can be played with other participants from anywhere in the world. They all just jump on an online network tied to the game. The influence on children today is not just their circle of friends, but their Internet "friends" as well when gaming.

I have been training Gary the martial arts since he was a baby. His training has included punches and kicks, knife defense, gun safety, how to survive a school shooting, and a lot of lectures about what he can and cannot do in the eyes of the law. He can recite the moral responsibilities of self-defense, because I have taught him well. Whenever we had played video war games together I was persistent to explain to him the difference between murder and justifiable homicide, such as when a police officer has to shoot a criminal or when a soldier fires upon an enemy combatant. My philosophy was, and is, that if he's going to play these games, which his father allows him to do, whether openly or in secret with his friends, then I'm going to at least offer him moral lessons along with the games.

When it comes to games like Grand Theft Auto, where players actually score points by injuring or killing citizens purposely, a very sick concept to say the least, I tell Gary that I will be very disappointed in him if he ever plays such games; the senseless violence ones. Granted, I don't feel particularly comfortable having him play war games either; for I'd much rather have him maintain his innocence, but one day he may have to defend my country. After all, there is long list of hostile countries preparing their children to destroy "the Great Satan," the United States of America. Some of these countries are even sending their young people to my soil regularly to slaughter my fellow citizens by doing bombings, shootings, stabbings, and other types of murder. Therefore, as Ecclesiastes 3:8 in the Bible states, there is "a time for war and a time for peace." Running innocent people over with a car or beating up a prostitute for points is evil, but I can't tell my nephew that war is always wrong, because sometimes it is necessary. As a former American soldier I took up arms to protect my generation, and I fully expect this generation to have the guts enough to protect my aging generation, and their children to come. There has not been world peace in 6,000 years of man's recorded history, and I don't suspect that there will be anytime soon. All I have to do is pull up the news on the T.V. or on the Internet to confirm that reality. That stated, I stand firmly against war crimes, such as "humping" a fallen soldier, even if he or she is only a cyber image made up of pixels. Violent video games do indeed condition young impressionable minds. If they didn't, then why does the United States Army produce their own combat video games, such as *America's Army*, for the country's youth, and look for potential recruits at gaming tournaments? Someone has to pilot our drones to hit isolated terrorist targets or physically step onto the next battlefield. Someone in the U.S. Space Force has to remotely pilot our killer satellites so that enemy countries don't park their killer satellites next to our many infrastructure satellites, and blow them up to disrupt our communication signals or shut down our electrical grid. Someone has to board vessels entering our territorial waters…

Forget all the university psych courses! One of the best educations in the world to really understand troubled youth is to be a law enforcement patrol officer where you get to go into peoples homes, or see kids on the streets taking out their aggressions. This is where I learned the connection between violent video games and violent music and violent crimes committed by young people. I've been in countless teenagers' rooms, and have rifled through their personal effects before taking them into custody. The small percentage of those that these negative forces do have an influence on, and where they want to take the fantasy to the next level, are the ones that get their hands on a gun and end up doing a school shooting. But it is not always with firearms. There is an increasing amount of stabbings by youths in recent years, and not just in the United States, but all over the world.

What? Are we going to outlaw all pointed knives to solve this problem? Is it the tool's fault? No, of course not. It's a matter of the heart.

The correlation of violent video games and violent music is much like the telltale signs of a rapist or child molester. Often times these predators started their appetite with pornography. That's not to say that everyone who stimulates their sexual lust with pornography is going to commit a sexual crime, man's laws anyway, nor does it mean that every child who plays violent shoot-em-up games to stimulate their bloodlust is going to end up on a murder spree, but some of those without self-control do. As the old proverb goes, "So as you think, you are." Or, to put it in computer jargon, "Data in, data out." The data you program into a computer will be the data that will come out. Letting children play violent video games without any responsible moral guidelines from concerned adults can lead to the creation of heartless, sociopath killers, and it seems like the past couple of decades has produced a lot of them, and there are inevitably more to come.

If you know any children playing violent games then it is your, not somebody else's, responsibly to put a stop to it, or give the proper moral guidance should they continue to play. The schools are not going to do it. The government is not going to do it. It's up to you to do it, and in so doing you may not only be possibly saving the life of that child one day, but potential victims as well. Even if that kid is not the type to go out and inflict damage upon others, your counseling contributes positively to their critical thinking.

Training for a violent world.

The student above (in the helmet) is protecting his principal perfectly by lining up his centerline with the principal's centerline. However, in the inset photo the principal (the light shirt) is almost entirely exposed to the gunman as they flee the attack.

Day 18

Principal Evacuation While Under Fire

Most traditional-based martial artists think that protecting someone is simply getting between the person they are protecting and the attacker while using their fighting skills. That may work fine in a bar fight, or other low-risk ego conflicts, but what about when the attacker is firing a gun at you and the person you are protecting, and you are well out of disarming distance? Most martial arts schools don't teach their students such advanced techniques and tactics.

In my Crime Survival course I teach my students actual bodyguard techniques and tactics used around the world by secret service agencies and bodyguard companies. After all, it is part of my professional tactical history: protecting diplomats, celebrities, and high-ranking military officers.

One bodyguard technique that every martial artist should know is the Principal Evacuation While Under Fire. The steps are as follows:

1. Place your primary hand (you learned all about the primary hand on Day 2) on back of the principal's neck, which protects the neck while at the same time can be used to "steer" the principal in the desired direction. Make sure your forearm protects the spine of the principal.

2. Place the secondary hand on the principal's stomach and bend him or her over so that their head is just below your shoulder level. Too little, and their head is not protected. Too much, and they won't be able to move fast.

3. Place your body directly behind the principal's, centerline to centerline, to "catch" any bullets or fragmentation from hitting them, and start moving.

4. Give commands to the principal as to where you want him or her to go, and obviously go the opposite way of the attack.

5. Move away from the attack using a combat glide (a fast tactical walk rolling the feet heel to toe), so as not to trip. Tripping and falling only keeps you in the Hot Zone longer.

6. Get the principal behind cover (a large object that stops bullets, fragmentation, or chemical agents) or to a Warm Zone (a dangerous area,

but not in the immediate Kill Zone), and then eventually to a Cold Zone (a safe area away from all danger).

7. If you are wounded, and unable to continue with the evacuation, instruct the principal to get to safety on his or her own. Your job will be slow down or stop the attack if possible when left behind.

Obviously there is a lot more to evacuating a principal, such as during a grenade or chemical attack, or whether you have firearms yourself, but at least you have enough information here to protect someone with your own body and get them out of the Hot Zone; also known as the Kill Zone.

Training for a violent world.

EVACUATION MOVEMENT

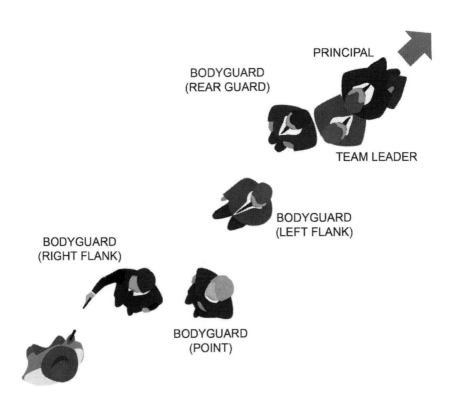

This is a diagram taken from a bodyguard manual that I wrote in 2014. It shows a 5-person Executive Protection team evacuating the principal from a gunman.

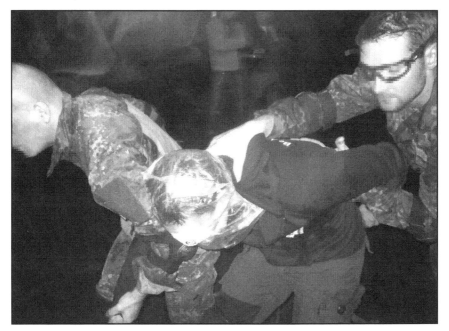

You must train for your reality. My students here, bodyguards in the German Army, are evacuating a "general," wearing a protective mask, from a chemical attack.

Due to the increasing attacks on faith-based organizations worldwide, I have taught many church security officers how to evacuate pastors, priests, and guest speakers.

Someone can collide into the back of your car because they were texting, unable to stop in time due to inclement weather, or did it on purpose. Some criminals make it look like a minor accident in order to get you out of the car, and then attack you.

Day 19

Head back! Head back! Head back!

When I was going through the U.S. Army's HUMVEE driving course, we had to learn how to yell, "Roll Over! Roll Over! Roll Over!" three times, should the vehicle ever start to roll, which can happen on a military base, public road, or on the battlefield. In addition, I was also taught to yell out, "Water! Water! Water!" if the vehicle was going to end up going into deep water. The military teaches soldiers these commands to warn everyone in the vehicle to brace for the catastrophe about to come. In fact, many warnings for combat are yelled out three times, such as "Gas! Gas! Gas!" to warn soldiers of a weaponized chemical agent attack.

Well, I came up with my own driving warning command for civilian situations, and it is this, "Head back! Head back! Head back!" And, it means exactly that. If I am stationary at a stop sign or at a red light, and in my rearview mirror I see a car or truck coming up behind me, and it is apparent that the driver is not going to stop and is going to collide into the back of my vehicle, I need to warn my passengers of the impending impact. The greatest risk to me and my passengers in such a situation, is a neck injury when the head snaps backwards as the impact sends my vehicle forward. With my technique, a whiplash injury is avoidable.

If I see in my review mirror that a collision is imminent, and I cannot move out of the way in time, then I yell out loudly, "Head back! Head back! Head back!" Upon this command my passengers are to quickly put the back of their heads onto the headrest behind them, and look straight ahead. This will brace the head as much as possible in the few moments that they have before impact. It minimizes the movement of the neck and spine when the car is launched forward.

This is not something you need to practice every week, but at least a few times a year. When you practice it by yourself, do it while at a stop. If you are with your trained family, friends, or coworkers, yell out the command to keep them in practice. Kids love doing this, and sometimes when you're not expecting it they like to yell out, "Head back! Head back! Head back! to see if you'll do it, and of course, you will.

Training for a violent world.

You could end up on the ground in this same position (man in the white shirt) where the attack is coming from the side. There are only 10 directions in the universe.

Here I am practicing techniques from my left side as my training partner braces the striking mannequin. After 15 seconds, I then flip onto my right side to practice.

Day 20

Ground fighting on your side

How many directions can you be attacked from? The answer is 10 different angles: front, back, horizontal left or right, vertical up or down, and four diagonal directions, which is essentially the letter "X." That makes 10 directions in total. This means there are only 10 directions someone can come at you with a knife, 10 directions someone can punch at you or kick at you, and 10 directions for movement to advance on the attacker or retreat from him: 8 directions on the ground, and up and down. The same holds true when you are fighting on the ground. There are 10 directions from which to fight.

Although the majority of martial arts schools teach their students how to fight an opponent who is mounted on you, either on top of your front or on your back, most don't teach their students how to fight from their sides, the horizontal component, and yet it can happen in a real fight. To get my students used to fighting on their sides, I have a drill where I use a striking mannequin or a punching bag, and a trainer is on his or her side supporting it. The trainer braces the striking mannequin with his or her knees on the lower portion while pushing the upper half with the hands, but placed in such a way as not to get hit. On the command of "Go!" I have the student strike the target with any techniques they want for 15 seconds. I yell out, "I want you to strike him with your feet, your knees, your elbows, your fists! Do whatever you can to win!" After the 15 seconds they roll onto their opposite side, and the clock starts again.

My original training drill helps the student learn to be comfortable fighting from their side. It teaches them that if they want effective hand or elbow strikes they had better rotate into the strike using torque to generate power. It teaches them that if they want to kick or knee the enemy they had better move their whole body into the strike to make it effective. Not only is this drill good for learning how to strike from a horizontal position, but it is a good endurance exercise as well. The only way you learn how to fight from your side is to do it, and in so doing you make your training that much more reality-based.

Training for a violent world.

In the inset photo both the Union forces, on the left, and the Confederate forces are arranged in *line of battle* formations firing upon each other. The large photo shows a Union infantry soldier with a socket bayonet fixed to a Springfield rifle.

Day 21

A system stuck in the past?

During the American Civil War, 1861–1865, most infantry battles were fought as you see in the inset photo. Armies would face each other in open fields in formations called "line of battle," which were long lines of soldiers standing shoulder to shoulder. Today such tactics seem suicidal, but back then this tactic was modern, and very much necessary.

During the Civil War, pistols and rifles shot lead musket balls or projectiles called "minié balls," invented in 1847. The rifle was the most common weapon in the Civil War. Most rifles were muzzle loaded, and it took approximately 20 to 30 seconds to reload and fire a second round. Therefore, while the soldiers who had just shot their load were reloading their rifles, the next row moved up and fired their weapons, and this cycle was repeated. To destroy the enemy, who advanced in human waves, concentrated musket fire was needed, thus the "line of battle" was the most practical fighting tactic at the time. There were no radios back in those days, therefore bugles and drums were the best form of communications that they had. This helped to keep troops together in order to effectively maneuver on the battlefield, delivering frontal and flanking attacks; not to mention that these black powder weapons also produced a lot of smoke on the battlefield, which often obstructed visibility.

Over time, with the creation of more efficient weapons, the line of battle tactic had become obsolete. Today's rifles can spray out a lot of bullets within a minute, and the effective range of an infantry rifle is 600 meters or more. One soldier can be extremely lethal against multiple targets. Therefore, the line of battle used in the American Civil War does not work today. Modern soldiers maneuver in smaller groups, they make use of cover and concealment, and they engage the enemy at greater distances. If today's soldiers come under fire in the open, and there is no available cover, they are trained to go to the ground and return fire.

It is fair to say that most techniques and tactics used in the American Civil War are not used today by the United State military. However, not all techniques and tactics of yesteryear have disappeared completely. For example, Civil War rifles were designed to have bayonets affixed to them that protruded beyond the muzzle as seen in the large photo. This was a stabbing weapon used for hand-to-hand combat when the weapon ran out of ammunition. Thrusting the sharp piece of metal into a human body is no different today than it was over a hundred and fifty years ago. Today's modern military rifles are still equipped with bayonets. Even in the future, when firearms will fire deadly lasers, bayonets will be needed if the "batteries" die. Although ancient bayonets differ in appearance, shape, and size, the function is exactly the same as today.

The point that I am trying to make, pun intended, is that just because a traditional-based martial arts system may have within it a technique or two that will work in a real fight, it does not mean that the system as a whole is valid when it comes to your self-defense training. Notice, I stated "self-defense," and not the other reasons that people study, or are seeking, a traditional-based martial art system, which may be for historical, cultural, or education purposes.

Yes, just like a Civil War bayonet technique, a good Karate punch slammed into somebody's face is as effective today as it was back in medieval Japan when samurai warriors did it. However, outdated katas (solo imaginary choreographed fights), which take a lot of time to learn, do nothing to prepare you for an active shooter incident. A Tae Kwon Do front kick to the groin is still valid today, like it was in 1861, but if a police officer or soldier were instructed today to do a head kick or a spinning back kick, when their life is in jeopardy no less, they'd believe their instructor to be crazy. Getting into very awkward fighting stances and doing acrobatic moves, like many Kung-fu systems teach, merely because of the traditions handed down from one generation to the next, is never even talked about in today's U.S. Army Combatives (hand-to-hand combat system). Some techniques and tactics just no longer work on today's battlefield, or even against today's criminals and terrorists for that matter. So, if self-defense is your objective, then you must go to instructors or systems that teach 100% modern self-defense, otherwise it is like trying to learn modern warfare by joining a Civil War reenactment club, which is how I got the photos you saw two pages ago.

Conversely, just because a traditional or sport-based system is not geared towards modern self-defense, it does not mean that you won't be able to extract some techniques and tactics that will work today in a real fight. As long as you know how to filter out the superfluous content, through your warrior wisdom, you'll find exactly what you are looking for.

Training for a violent world.

The American Civil War *line of battle* formation is obsolete today. Modern weapons have changed the tactics of warfare, as shown by these soldiers of my former Military Police unit. However, using a modern bayonet has not changed at all.

A woman in my Knife Expert course in Dawlish, England throws a rubber training knife (seen in midair) at a mannequin in a traditional-based self-defense school. The inset photo shows a German student about to throw an actual throwing knife.

Day 22

There are only 3 situations for throwing a knife

Most knives are not designed for throwing. There are throwing knives, which are perfectly balanced for the task, but in most countries they are illegal to carry in your vehicle or on your person. If you are caught with a throwing knife the police will automatically arrest you, unless you work for a circus as a knife thrower and are on your way there. It is more likely that you are going to defend yourself with a pocket knife, provided they are legal to carry in your jurisdiction, or a kitchen knife if you find yourself being attacked in a restaurant or in your own home. These knives are not designed for throwing.

Hollywood movies make knife throwing, of any knife it seems, look so easy to do. In an action film the knife is thrown with great skill, and it always seems to find its target point first. The imbedded knife even brings the bad guy down, like a rifle bullet would. However, in real life that rarely happens, especially with a tactical folder or a steak knife. Anyone who has ever gone out in the backyard and thrown knives at a wood plank or a tree knows how difficult it is to stick a knife point first, and when the distance is changed ever so slightly, the learning curve starts all over again in order to find the perfect amount of rotations it takes to stick it.

The general rule is NEVER GIVE UP YOUR WEAPON. If a knife is all you have to defend yourself then it is more effective tightly secured with a fist grip in your hand, and with it you will stab and slash when the attacker is in your Red Zone (within touching distance). A knife is a close range weapon, and a very lethal one at that. Throwing it at an attacker has a lot of negative aspects associated with it: you get rid of your weapon, you possibly give your attacker a weapon to be used against you, you may miss, and it may not strike point first. Even if it does stick, it may not go deep enough to penetrate a vital organ.

There are only three situations for throwing a knife at an attacker:

1. You want to injure your attacker as he is coming at you, but you have

another weapon as a back up in case it doesn't work.

2. You are running away from the attacker, and you want to slow him down so that you can escape; be it getting over a fence, into your car, or through a door and locking it behind you. Suddenly turning and throwing any object at someone, especially a sharp knife, can slow them down. This was the reason that ancient Japanese ninjas (assassins) concealed shurinkens (small flat metal "stars" with pointed tips) in a leather pouch. If a ninja were being pursued on foot by samurai, or enemy soldiers, they'd grab a hand full of these throwing stars from their pouch, turn, and send them sailing all at once. The enemy hand no choice but to try to dodge them or get injured, thus giving the ninja a few extra precious seconds to escape.

3. You have been seriously injured, you can't escape, and the attacker is coming up to you to execute you. In this case this will be your last resort; your last ditch effort to survive. Even if you don't stop him, you're at least trying to injure him to give him a scar to remember you by. You're going to die anyway, so it's worth a try.

When I teach my 8-hour Knife Expert course I have a portion devoted to knife throwing techniques and tactics. I have my students throw a variety of knives, which includes professional throwing knives; even throwing stars (shurikens) where it is legal to do so. I always tell my students, "Your throw is a success if you strike the target with any part of the knife, be it with the handle, side of the knife, and especially the tip. As long as you hit him there is a chance of injury. Don't buy into the lie of Hollywood that you are going to stick it perfectly, and the attacker is going to go down."

Once in a while the point goes in first with a folding knife or a kitchen knife, but it is quite rare, and when it does happen all of the students cheer. This is the reason the course is called Knife Expert, and that is because an expert in self-defense should know how to throw a knife.

After my students gave a few knives a try I have them do it again with their opposite hand (the secondary hand), and few people can't even hit the human sized target at all. So, the lesson there is always throw the knife with your primary hand. It is not even worth the time and effort to train your secondary hand. As I explained to you on Day 2 in the Jim Wagner Reality-Based Personal Protection system there is no such thing as a "weak hand." Many martial arts systems don't call it that, but by calling the primary hand the "strong hand," that can only mean the opposite for the other hand, and words are powerful, and I don't want my students thinking they have a weak anything.

The only way you are going to discover these "truths of combat," when it comes to throwing knives, is to try it yourself. Get a human length wood plank, set it up vertically, and throw different types of knives at it from various distances. You'll discover very soon what could injure an attacker and what definitely won't. Remember safety, and always wear eye protection in case of bounce back. Sometimes a knife can bounce back all the way to your throwing position; I've seen it many times.

Oh, and one more thing. Sometimes when I teach knife throwing I find myself in a facility where it is not possible to throw real knives. Some really nice traditional-based or sport-based schools don't want a real knife putting holes in their walls or in their mats, or City Hall employees don't want real knives in their building at all. In this case I'll simulate these three techniques with rubber or plastic knifes. I'll have them run away from the attacker, be it an instructor in protective gear or a striking mannequin, to the proper throwing range distance, and then the student will suddenly turn and hurl the training knife at the target, and then start running away again. If anything, it teaches the proper throwing distance, and tests their accuracy. When I have them all try again with their secondary hand, watch out! The training knives fly ever which way. When training for technique number 3 I'll have the attacker, armed with a rubber training firearm or an Airsoft firearm, walk up to the "victim," who is "wounded" on the ground, or set up the striking mannequin at the proper distance, and the student will do their last defiant act – throw the knife at the executioner.

Training for a violent world.

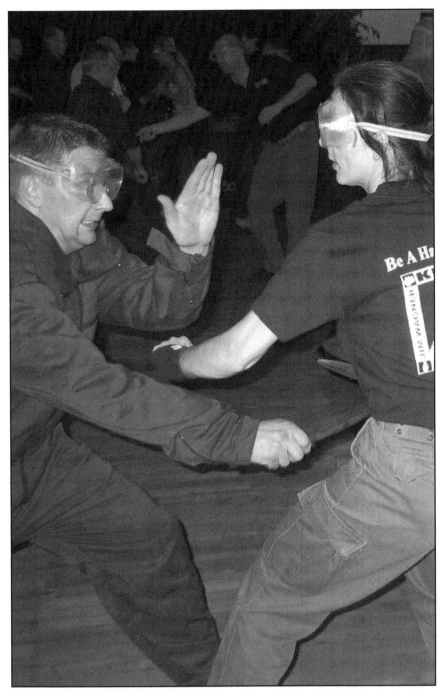

The student on the right just got stabbed in the gut during a realistic scenario. When this happens many students immediately give up thinking that they are "dead." I yell at such students, "Keep going! Keep going! You're only injured!"

Day 23

"Keep going! You're only injured!"

That's what I yell out to my students who feel like giving up just after they got stabbed with a rubber training knife or shot with a 6mm Airsoft projectile.

Even after a scenario, when the "injuries" would be catastrophic, I tell my students, "You're not dead until a paramedic or doctor declares you dead, or you feel yourself leaving your body and you are heading to a bright light at the end of the tunnel. Until then, keep going! You are only injured, and not dead."

I've seen many martial arts instructors over the years say to their students after a critical injury in a training scenario, "You're dead!" Yes, the well-meaning instructor is trying to convey a message to their students that they must improve their skills to avoid being killed in a real fight, but unfortunately injuries are sometimes the result of physical conflict. Who's to say that a wound is fatal or not? I let my students know from the start that in a fight they may get hurt, but they must mentally prepare for that eventuality and overcome it.

The problem with telling a student, "You're dead!" in a training scenario is that the mind is very powerful, and if they do get stabbed or shot in a real conflict one day, even if the injuries may not be life threatening, the mind has been reinforced by the bad instructor's messaging. They've been told that they are dead, and so they just very well may be. They have associated getting shot or stabbed in training with death. It's no wonder they may give up hope.

On the other hand, reinforcing students with the words, "Keep going! Keep going! You're only wounded! You can keep fighting!" is a Jump Start Command, *a command given while the training is in progress in order for the student to do the right thing*, that will stay in their mind for a lifetime, and it will be what drives them on in a real conflict even if they are seriously injured. Continuing to fight, even if injured, does not always mean staying toe-to-toe with the bad guy and enduring more punishment, but it also could mean continuing the fight by escaping. Continuing the fight means that the student has fled to a Warm Zone, a safer area away from the conflict, and tend to their injuries and get on the phone in order to get the police and ambulance rolling their way. *He that fights and runs away, may turn and fight another day; But he that is in battle slain, will never rise to fight again. Tacitus*

Likewise, I always correct my students who blurt out, "I'm dead!" after they have been stabbed or shot in a scenario. I am quick to respond, "No, you're not dead! You are only wounded. Yes, you need to stop the bleeding now with direct pressure, and then go get patched up in a hospital, but you're not dead." When I say this you can see in their eyes the shift from defeat to the hope of survival.

Words are powerful, and instructors must always keep this in mind when teaching their students realistic self-defense.

Now, could a self-defense practitioner be fatally wounded in a real fight and die? Of course they can. That is always a possibility, but an instructor should not contribute to a possible future defeat, but instead instill in their students the "will to survive."

So what about those who don't have an instructor? Perhaps it's just you and your training partner. Well, guess what? You are your own coach. If you get stabbed or shot during your training scenario you must tell yourself, "No problem! I can take 100 stab wounds, or 100 bullets!" That's what I've come to believe when I am doing realistic scenarios. Therefore, if I only get stabbed three times I will say to myself, "I can take 97 more."

Obviously, I'm not out of touch with reality. I'm fully aware that a single stab from a knife or one bullet from a firearm can finish me if it hits a critical spot. On the other hand, as a former police officer I have come to the aid of victims who have had multiple stab wounds or multiple gunshot wounds, and they survived.

A defining moment in my life is when, as a police officer, I responded to the apartment of a man who called the police after a "friend" had stabbed him 9 times in the chest and abdomen. When I arrived he was laying in a large pool of blood in his living room. I just assumed that he been stabbed only a minute or two before my arrival, because I had been just down the street when the call came out. When I didn't find the suspect, the victim told me that he had been laying there for 30 minutes. When I asked him what took him so long to call he said, "I didn't think it was serious."

This man, who was bleeding to death for 30 minutes, didn't think his injuries were "serious!" Then I thought to myself, *If this idiot can survive nine stab wounds, then so can I, but more."* And, so can you.

Training for a violent world.

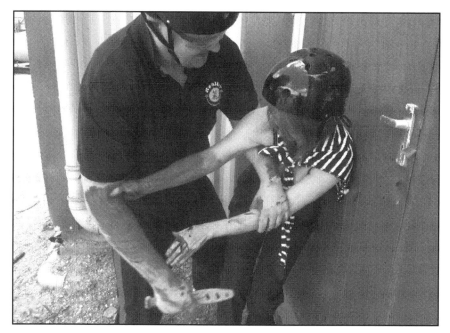

Despite getting cut and stabbed multiple times (it's only stage blood) in this brutal knife attack in Carrickmacross, Ireland this woman refused to give up.

In a situation like this, where terrorists shoot everyone in sight, you may have to "play dead" if you are wounded, just like these students at the University of Paris.

107

Imagine walking in on this scene with a dead woman, and a man screaming with a gun in his hand. You'd look upon it and experience tunnel vision (visual exclusion).

That's me in 1990 with the two actors from the above scene. One of my duties was setting up realistic scenarios for my S.W.A.T. team to "open up" their tunnel vision.

Day 24

You will experience tunnel vision

After you have finished a roll of toilet paper, or you come to the end of the paper towels, save the cardboard tube that the paper came off of. This is an excellent teaching tool to help you understand the Conflict Perceptual Distortion phenomena known among tactical operators as "tunnel vision" (also known as *visual exclusion*). Hold one end of the tube up to your eye and look around the room with it. Needless to say your field of vision is going to be very limited. You still will be able to see clearly those things you are looking at directly, but everything outside of the "target zone" is not going to be part of your sight picture. Hold up that same cardboard tube just as you start a realist self-defense scenario, and you'll get some idea of what tunnel vision is like in real combat.

Whenever you get into a physical fight YOU WILL experience one or more psychological changes that will influence you physically. One of those changes during a life and death conflict that will always be present is tunnel vision, and you can't avoid it. As if looking through that cardboard tube, your vision will be focused on the immediate threat, and excluding other visual cues just outside of the focus point. To a small degree you can experience tunnel vision in a sparring match in a martial arts school or inside the ring of an MMA match, but it will not be as acute as when your safety is really at stake (serious bodily injury or death). The more the danger, the more narrow the tunnel becomes.

Most traditional-based or sport-based martial arts instructors do not tell their students that they will experience tunnel vision, simply because most martial arts instructors lack real world conflict experience. They've never had someone try to seriously injure them or kill them with a knife, a gun, or with bare hands. Those instructors who have been in real combat tend to teach the psychological aspects of combat right along with the physical techniques. Therefore, if you have never been in a life-and-death fight before, you are going to have to trust me that you will experience tunnel vision. Then, when the time comes that you do experience it, you are not going to panic and think that something strange is happening to you. It is perfectly normal.

If you are a self-defense instructor, who has never experience tunnel vision before, you have an obligation to teach your students that this phenomena will manifest in a real fight, and perhaps you can best explain it by handing out a cardboard tube to each student and explaining the phenomena that way; just like I explained it to you in the opening paragraph. There's nothing better when making a point than by having a hands-on demonstration.

Although you will experience tunnel vision in a real fight you can certainly "open up" that tunnel to see more things. It doesn't have to be narrow. Enlarging that tunnel is accomplished through realistic training and actual experience. The first time someone tried to kill me, admittedly, my tunnel (my psychological and physical field of vision) was very narrow - almost pinpoint. However, after several more incidents, and a lot of intense realistic self-defense training, the tunnel has expanded over the years contributing to my survival. However, the tunnel vision has never completely gone away, nor will it ever when confronted with serious injury or death. The larger tunnel that I am now subjet to look through will allow me see more details in a conflict.

I know that I sound repetitive, but realistic training means just that - **realistic**. In order to remotely experience any kind of tunnel vision, your self-defense training has to parallel real-life attacks that you may face. In order to do that, you need a realistic attacker (someone who is following a script, acting like the real thing, and dressed in the attire that a real attacker would be wearing). In addition, you need a realistic environment (a theatrical stage, as it were, with props, sights and sounds) it possible.

Training for a violent world.

So realistic were my scenarios, along with the effective techniques and tactics that I taught, that police departments around the world hired me to train their instructors.

Civilians need the same realism in training as the police, and I introduced it to the civilian martial arts community in 2003, like this realistic bank takeover scenario.

111

The clerk was just shot by the robber in this convenience store, and he turns his gun next on a customer. Taking advantage of the robber being distracted, the female customer (a student) runs for the exit during this scenario in Dallas, Texas.

Day 25

Tactical retreat

Sometimes the roles get reversed. My beginners know what to do, and those who are supposedly "trained" in the martial arts don't. Let me give you a prime example.

I have a Knife Survival drill called Knife Avoidance. A "homeless man" approaches the unarmed student in the "street" asking for a little money. When the student tells him that he or she has no money to give, the man flies into a rage and attacks his victim with a rubber knife. Even after I have instructed all of the students that "distance is your friend" in a knife fight, most of the trained martial artists want to stand their ground and fight, whereas the beginners have no problem running away. It's common sense. The reason that most martial artisits want to stay and fight an attacker with a knife, even though few of them survive such a fight, is because that's the way they've been trained. Hence, *You fight as you train.*

A lot of martial artists, because they have been conditioned to always stay and fight no matter what, believe it is cowardly to turn and run. Not so in police or military training. Sometimes professionals have no choice, but we don't call it "running," we call it a "tactical retreat." Therefore, running should be a part of your self-defense training. I'm not talking about long distance running, but sprinting short distances that allows you enough time to deploy your weapon, or to get out of the Hot Zone. For example, in a knife fight you may have to sprint 21 feet (7 meters) to give you enough seconds to get out your tactical pen or tactical flashlight (torch) from your pocket, and be ready to strike with it. Or, during an active shooter incident you may have to run down a hallway and into a room to get away from the shooter who is hunting people down. That distance could possibly be half the length of a football field.

Sometimes the easiest and cheapest methods are the best. It takes very little time, and no money, to go outside and run as fast as you can 50 to 100 meters. I do this every other day. Such conditioning not only prepares you to get away as fast as possible, a tactical retreat, but it also regulates your breathing when you are using maximum energy in a fight.

Training for a violent world.

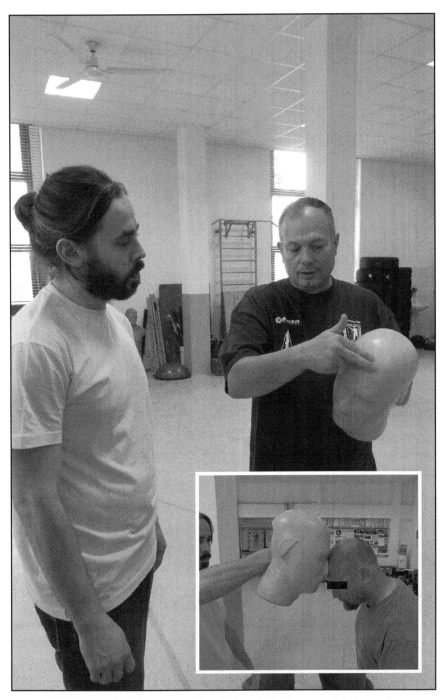

In a self-defense school in Prague, Czech Republic, I am explaining to instructor Mario Tacheci how to do a proper head butt strike. The only way this strike can hit the target is if the victim has his hands down, leaving his head unprotected.

Day 26

Head Butt Avoidance

Most men get head butted right in the face simply because they don't know how to stand tactically when a hostile man is right up in their face. The worse position you can put yourself in is having your hands down, puffing out your chest (posturing), and letting your big ego override your common sense. It's no wonder many thugs take advantage of this un-prepared position in a bar fight when getting into a pissing match out in public, and then smash the unsuspecting victim right between the horns.

The general rule to avoid a head butt attack is to keep your hands up high in front of you, and expect the attack.

Anytime someone is close to you, especially an argumentative person, you must "talk with your hands." You need to keep your two hands up high in front of you and make them look natural, as opposed to looking defensive. You can rub your hands together, make gestures, play with your ring while saying, "Hey look, I don't want any trouble," and don't allow the aggressor to get too close to you. The raised hands serve as both a physical and psychological barrier that your opponent must get past in order to head butt you. Without your "shield" you're defenseless.

In my one-day Defensive Tactics course I cover Head Strikes, also known as "head butts," towards the end of the course. I teach my students a wide variety of head strikes from around the world. After everyone has practiced these techniques I always ask my class, "Is there anyone here who has ever done a head butt against someone in a real fight?" I usu-ally get a few hands that shoot up. I then select one of them, usually the biggest and meanest of the bunch, and I tell him, "I want you to come up to me and really head butt me. When you do it try to knock me out. I'm serious."

None of my students have ever come close to head butting me, because I keep my hands up high in front of me, and if they get too close I push them away from me. Yes, I know, it's "too simple." That's the whole idea, and that's what it takes to deal with this type of attack. Sometimes the simplest techniques work the best.

Training for a violent world.

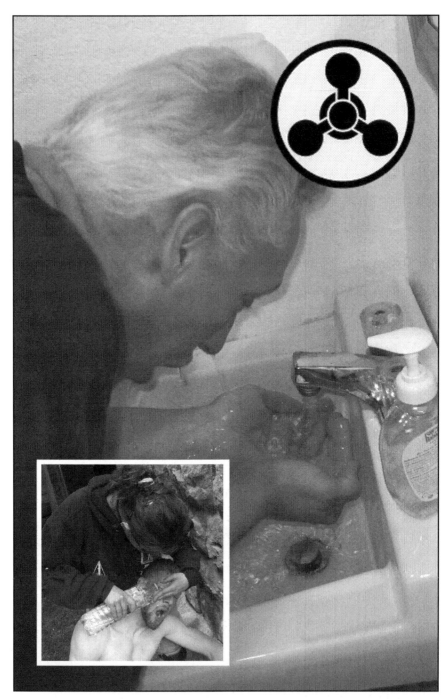

In some of my Terrorism Survival courses, depending on what country I'm in, I will pepper spray my students to give them an idea of the horrors of a chemical attack. Here two different students are going through the decontamination process.

Day 27

CHEMICAL DECON

Do you live in a large city or are you planning to visit one anytime soon? Los Angeles, New York City, Chicago, Paris, you name it. A terrorist chemical attack is always a possible event that you should anticipate, and it's a catastrophic event you should train for. After all, every major city in the world has first responders (police, fire, and medical), and selected military units, ready to respond to a chemical attack.

What does a chemical attack look like? How will you recognize one if it happens? There are several ways that terrorists could disperse a deadly toxin. One way is to have a conventional explosive charge burst open a container filled with a liquid chemical. The contents of the ruptured container are instantly released into the environment. The telltale signs of this type of attack are the sound of an explosion followed by a chemical cloud (plume) where people experience eye irritation, choking, or collapsing near the proximity of the blast; or downwind of the blast. Another way to disperse chemical agents is by aerosolizing it (forming particles small and light enough to be carried on the air) by means of a crop duster (an airplane that sprays pesticides on crops), aerosol dispenser, or the terrorists may have even obtained a military artillery shell containing a deadly toxin. However, a chemical attack is not limited to the outdoors where a lot of people are concentrated. A deadly chemical agent can be released in the ventilation system of a building. Obviously, some buildings are more likely targets than others, such as government buildings, sporting events, political rallies, a national museum, synagogues, et cetera. If you are in a building, never go to the basement, because weaponized chemicals in a gaseous state are heavier than air. They flow like water does.

If you are ever the victim of a terrorist chemical attack don't rely on the first responders to help you, because they may not be able to get to you in time. You must be able to survive on your own until you get medical attention, and here's the decontamination (DECON for short) procedure you will follow.

1. In a designated area, well away from the Hot Zone, you will be stripped of your clothing, which eliminates as much as 80-90% of the contamination, and then sprayed with a high volume of water with low

pressure for a minimum of 30 seconds, but no longer than 3 minutes. This may be done by way of Ladder Pipe Decontamination System (LDS), basically walking between two fire engines parallel to each other that spray a corridor of water from hoses on both sides, or walking through a large tent with water nozzles above. You go inside one end, and out the other.

2. You will be scrubbed down with a soap and water solution by a soft brush. This is the only way to get the fine particles off of you.

3. Your personal items will be decontaminated, bagged, and tagged.

4. You will be given clean clothes (usually a jumpsuit).

5. You will receive medical attention, and transported if needed.

What if there are mass casualties, and the government's recourses are spread thin? If you find yourself on your own you may have to do your own decontamination process, and here's how to do it:

1. Remove all your clothing, including shoes, because clothing will off gas for up to 30 minutes after contact with a nerve agent. Place them inside a "DECON bag," which is a sealable plastic bag.

2. Flush your skin and personal items (keys, cards, cash) with water - lots, and lots, of water. Since I live in Los Angeles I have a DECON kit in the trunk of my car that has a 1 gallon (4 liters) container of water to immediately pour over myself and a passenger. A second 1 gallon container is filled with water mixed with dishwashing soap to get the agent off of the skin and out of your hair. The Palmolive Dish Detergent brand was recommended to me by a Los Angeles HAZMAT firefighter in our Intermediate Terrorism Liaison Officer course, and that's what I use.

3. Have a soft scrub brush (like a vegetable brush) to scrub off the agent. With a third, and final gallon of water, rinse off the contaminated soap and water solution. Remember that the runoff water is going to be contaminated, and you must think of where the water is going to flow. Stepping in the contaminated water, and then walking to another location will track the chemical agent there. A child's inflatable pool works great to contain all the runoff, but this obviously involves some serious planning. It's something a bodyguard team might have in the trunk.

4. Put on some new clothes, and immediately seek medical attention.

This information alone is not enough. You need to practice the steps to make them *muscle memory*, and to test your DECON equipment. Then, once a year, revisit the training to maintain your skills.

Training for a violent world.

Getting attacked with an unknown liquid chemical agent, like this woman at Club Med Pompadour France, requires decontamination after fleeing the Hot Zone.

These are the men and women who would respond to a terrorist chemical attack in New York City. It is a U.S. Army unit prepared to go into a contaminated area.

Canadian Deputy Sheriff Mike Kendall is about to search a "suspect" for weapons in my Tactical Knife course, and he must complete the task within 60 seconds.

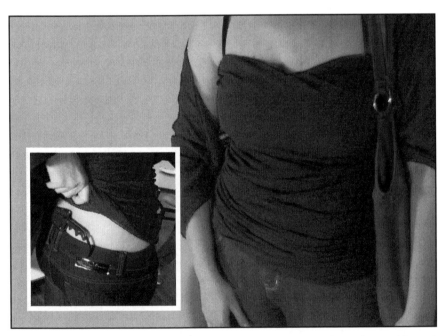

You'd think that most women would carry a knife in their purse. Well, not this one! She has a concealed fixed blade located at the small of her back under her blouse.

Day 28

Failure is a great teacher

Have you ever had to actually fight a criminal? Not some petty thief who stole a pack of cigarettes, but hard-core gang members, robbers, or people who were whacked out on drugs? I have, and that is how the Jim Wagner Reality-Based Personal Protection system evolved.

Before I became a police officer, I was a corrections officer working in the Costa Mesa Police Department Men's Jail Facility in Southern California, just south of Los Angeles, from 1988 to 1991.

Police officers would arrest criminals out on the streets, and then bring them into the jail where they were placed inside a booking cage to be searched. All their personal items, except their clothes, would be taken from them and then bagged and tagged. When the police officer was finished searching their prisoner for any weapons or contraband in the booking cage, it was then my responsibility to go into the booking cage and do a secondary search before bringing him or her out to be photographed and finger printed.

Most of the time the arresting officer was thorough with his or her search, but there were several times that I found drugs cleverly hidden in a prisoner's clothing. On occasion I would even find a small knife. Fortunately, I never found a firearm. If I did find a weapon I would discreetly let the officer know about it. A police officer could get into serious trouble with his or her supervisor if such a mishap was ever revealed.

I considered prisoner searches my greatest responsibility when I worked in the jail, because overlooking a concealed weapon could mean another inmate being injured or killed, or worse, a fellow corrections officer or me.

Of all the custody officers assigned to the jail, I was one of the most skilled at finding concealed contraband and weapons. I paid close attention to those police officers that did good searches, and I took their mentoring seriously. Conversely, I was appalled at those few police officers that did sloppy searches, and I learned what not to do from them.

The thousands of prisoner searches I did in the Costa Mesa Police Men's Jail eventually became part of the Jim Wagner Reality-Based Personal Protection system over a decade later, especially in my Tactical

Knife and Crime Survival courses.

Up until recently my Tactical Knife course was RESTRICTED to law enforcement, corrections, and military personnel. A few years ago I opened it up to instructors who have completed the Knife Survival Instructor and Expert Knife Survival Instructor courses since they'll inevitably end up teaching professionals that attend their courses. Anyway, at the tail end of the Tactical Knife course I have all the participants partner up. I then send half of them outside of the classroom for ten minutes so that they cannot see what I am doing with their partners. I then pull out a small cardboard box filled with all kinds of edged weapons: big and small, common and exotic. I hand three or four edged weapons to each "criminal" instructing them, "Conceal these on your person. However, hide them where they are easily accessible. Don't be shoving my clean knives up your rectum!" They all laugh. Not that they ever intend on placing one of them into a body cavity, but most of them do indeed think of putting them under their scrotum or under the sole of their foot inside one of their shoes just to give their partner a hard time. Relying on my teaching experience I stop them dead in their tracks before they go that far. Most real criminals will have an edged weapon cleverly concealed, but in a place where they can get to it easily in order to use against a fellow criminal or a police officer making contact with them. Many of my female students, playing the role of a "bad girl," have hidden blades in their bra between their breasts, but that area is easily accessible, and I have actually found weapons there many times when I arrested prostitutes.

I then call the "good guys" back into the room and have them face their training partners. I explain the rules, "When I say 'Go!' you have sixty seconds to search your prisoner. You can use whatever search method you want, and your 'bad guy' will be 100% cooperative. He will not resist you. Whatever you tell him to do, he will do. If you find a concealed weapon just set it aside and continue your search until you are finished searching the entire body or until I give the order to stop at the end of 60 seconds. Does everyone understand the training exercise?"

With much anxiety, giggling, and poker faces as weapons are missed during the several searches going on simultaneously, I check my stopwatch and then shout out, "Stop!" when it's time.

Most edged weapons are found, but a frightening large amount is always missed; even by seasoned cops. I then make those who missed a weapon or two drop down and give me ten push-ups for every one they missed. Out of the entire class only a couple of the students don't have to do the punishment, because they found every concealed weapon. The success or failure always depends on how much training and experience the searching students has.

My parting words in concluding this phase of Tactical Knife training is, "Remember what you saw here today, and how many edged weapons were never found. Be systematic like I taught you when we debriefed each search. For if you are not, you may never have the opportunity to do another search again, because you'll be dead!"

In my Crime Survival course for civilians I teach my students how to confront a burglar in their own home. A portion of the instructions that I give them, and only for very specific circumstances, includes how to bind and search the criminal for concealed weapons. I don't go into as much detail as I do with the professionals, because I don't give away trade secrets to civilians, but I do give them enough knowledge and techniques to keep them safe in their own "reality."

So, what is the moral of these stories? The moral is, *It is okay to fail in training*. Failing in training is survivable, but failing in the streets in a real conflict can get you severely injured or even getting your life taken from you, or worse, maybe losing the life of someone you care about that are supposed to protect. In addition, *Don't ever trust another person with your safety*. Unless I know a fellow operator has had extensive training and experience searching a detainee or a prisoner for weapons (all types of weapons), I won't trust their search. That means that I'll do a secondary search of the subject, even if it offends my partner, or if time and circumstances don't allow it, I'll keep a sharp eye on the subject until he or she is no longer a possible threat to me. Having handcuffs on somebody does not mean they are permanently restrained. The good guys often referred to prisons as "Universities for Criminals," because they're where criminals are educated to be better criminals. They teach each other how to get out of restraints, how to better hide weapons, and how to overpower a police officer.

Training for a violent world.

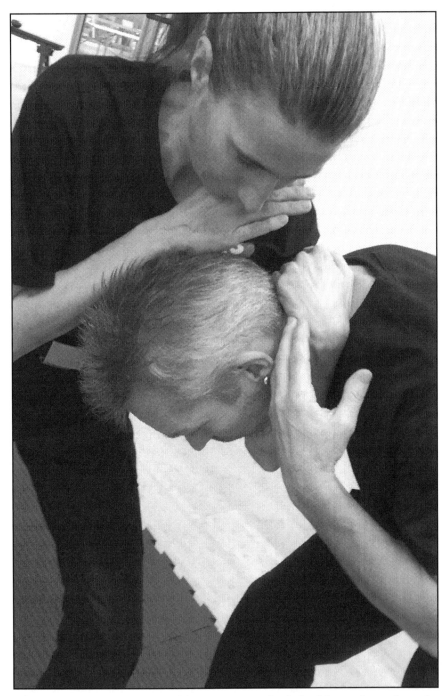

A martial artist over 40 years old may seem perfectly healthy, and may have the skills to perform any chokehold escape, but there is a tremendous danger associated with chokehold training. Warrior wisdom requires safeguards for this age group.

Day 29

The danger of practicing chokeholds

YOU COULD DIE PRACTICING CHOKEHOLDS! That's my stern warning to anyone over 40 years old.

The older you get, the more plaque that can build up in your arteries, especially for martial artists over 40 years old. For those of you who are under 40 years old this warning applies to you also, but in a different way. You may end up getting partnered up with someone that is over 40 years old during chokehold training, and you don't want to be the one responsible for the death of the older student. Nobody should ever die in training. It is completely unacceptable. Therefore, all martial artists need to take heed to this warning.

Any pressure, even slight pressure, on the neck of someone over 40 years old during chokehold training is dangerous, because once the pressure of the hold is released the blood that had been blocked in the carotid artery temporarily has more pressure behind it. To visualize the threat, it is like a dam on a river suddenly toppling over and more water rushing down the channel bringing with it rocks and debris from the bottom of the reservoir. The additional pressure caused by the release of the chokehold in training can dislodge some loose plaque, like the rocks and debris of a river, and go into the brain causing a massive stroke or other life threatening complications.

In my 8-hour course titled Control & Defense I teach a section titled Chokehold Defense; chokes from every possible attack direction, which, as you know, are 10. Before I start the chokehold training I read the warning disclaimer directly from the course outline, which everyone receives a current revised copy for proper training and courtroom documentation. It states:

WARNING: *Students over 40 years of age must not have any pressure applied to the neck due to the possibility of dislodging plaque and causing blood clots.*

I then tell all my students that, "absolutely no pressure is to be applied to any student over 40 years old." Essentially the older students only go through the motions in order to learn the techniques. For those under 40 years old I advise them to use their own discretion as to the amount of pressure they wish for their partner to apply to them. For example, an overweight person or a person with known heart disease may want to follow the NO PRESSURE ON THE NECK rule also. Communication between partners is essential for safe training.

I am over 50 years old, and I follow my own advice. When I need to demonstrate the defense against a particular chokehold I tell my partner, "Absolutely no pressure on my neck," and then I demonstrate the technique. I can't tell you how many times in the past I have trained where I actually wanted my partner to choke me out, but that was before I knew about the dangers of chokehold training, and having the information confirmed by the many medical professionals who have attended my courses over the years for various reasons: emergency room doctors, paramedics, and tactical medics. Interesting enough, in all of my real fights with criminals (for I was a street police patrol officer for many years, as you know) I never had a bad guy try to choke me. I've trained to survive the situation thousands of times over the years, but I never had to use these particular skills. Yet, because a chokehold is always a real possibility in a real conflict I needed to train to defeat them, and I still do to this day. Since I am over 50 years old I need to train smarter, and with proper safety protocols in place. Yes, I believe in reality-based training, but I don't believe in reality-based injuries or deaths in training.

I think of all of those Brazilian Ju-Jitsu, Greco-Roman wrestling, and MMA practitioners, including many of the instructors teaching these systems, who practice chokeholds and know nothing about this potential chokehold training danger, and as such I cringe at the very thought of a future training death. I'd like to try to prevent it, and I hope you do as well.

Training for a violent world.

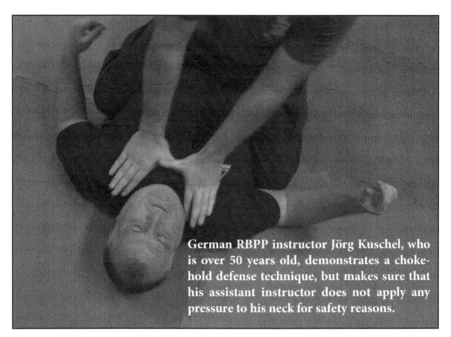

German RBPP instructor Jörg Kuschel, who is over 50 years old, demonstrates a chokehold defense technique, but makes sure that his assistant instructor does not apply any pressure to his neck for safety reasons.

It is the responsibility of the student who is over 40 years old to tell his training partner that he does not want any pressure applied to his neck for chokeholds.

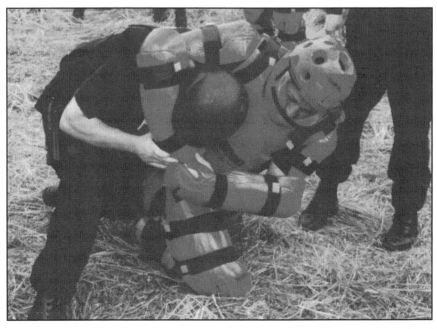

It is mandatory for self-defense instructors to warn students of the risks associated with chokehold training: age, being overweight, or previous medical conditions.

Even though the student on the left tried to block the pool noodle, coming in at full speed and full contact, with an instinctive block (arm up and hand open) he still missed it, and he would have got his ribs broken had this been a real stick or baton.

Day 30

The secret to blocking punches

Do you want to know the secret to blocking punches? Just attack someone with a foam pool noodle without warning. That's right, one of those children's long colorful pool noodles with a hole in the center, which you see in the stores just before summer. Cut it down to the size of a police baton, and then when they least expect it start beating them with it at full speed and full contact. You'll see the secret to blocking with your own eyes.

Blocking is instinctive. If you catch a glimpes of an object being thrown at you, say a beer bottle, rock, or a punch coming towards your face, you'd have only a split second to react. In that split second, without even thinking about it, you'd automatically shoot your arm (or arms), up in front of you toward the threat, with hands open, and without any conscious awareness of your arm angle, muscle tension, or form.

To illustrate this point with my students I bring out a pool noodle cut to size, and without warning I start trying to hit the selected student at full speed and full contact with it. I don't give him or her time to do some fancy block. I just come at them trying to hit an opening before they have a chance to block. It's always fast and furious. Regardless of their level of training, they block the incoming strikes with simple blocks, because they don't have time for anything else. There are no traps, fancy stances, beautifully formed arm angles, or any fine motor skill moves; it's just raw effective blocking. It's funny how children tend to naturally block the same way, and just as effectively as the adults do when I do this drill.

Not all blocks are instinctive though. Sometimes an attacker will telegraph their punch, which gives you time to think about the block you'd like to use. In that case, when your training takes over, it would be best to close the fist in order to tighten the muscles around the radius and ulna bones of the forearm in order to protect them from fracturing or breaking.

In a real fight you are only going to block once, maybe twice, and that 's only because you were caught by surprise. After that, you are either doing a tactical retreat or going on the offensive until you stop the attacker.

Training for a violent world.

That's my nephew Gary, 9 years old, sparring with a boy in a Karate tournament in Southern California. Gary had to learn, just like all of us must learn, to fight "without passion and without hatred." After all, emotions can contribute to defeat.

Day 31

"without hatred"

Au combat, tu agis sans passion et sans haine.
Code d'Honneur du Légionnaire

The translation from French to English is, "In combat, you act without passion and without hatred." I got it from the fifth paragraph of the first line of the French Foreign Legion Code of Honor.

The French Foreign Legion is a branch of the French Army established in 1831. The Legionnaires are highly trained infantry soldiers commanded by French officers with 76% of the enlisted soldiers being foreigners willing to fight for France, yet it is the only part of the French military that does not swear allegiance to France, but to the Foreign Legion for a minimum of five years. They are rugged, tough commandos with a strong *esprit de corps.*

Just a historical side note before I go on, and that is in December of 1985 I was in Paris on vacation by myself. I was young, single, spoke a little French, and I had a strong appetite for adventure. So, I looked up the address for the recruiting office for the French Foreign Legion and went to their Paris office. Although I had served in the United States Army, a big part of me wanted to join the Legionnaires. When I got there I saw an abandoned office with a hand written note on an A4 size sheet of paper taped to the window from the inside. The handwritten note stated that the recruiting office had moved to Marseille, 660 kilometers (410 miles) away in the south of France, and if anyone wanted to enlist they had to go down there. As I was walking back to my hotel room, quite disappointed, I bumped into two young Australian women, Heather and Teresa, who were backpacking across Europe, and who had just arrived in the city. I invited them to dinner, showed them the Eiffel Tower after the meal, and by the end of the evening I thought to myself, *These women are having the adventure of a lifetime, without joining the military. Do I want to sit in some African desert outpost for the next five years?* I had grown quite fond of sipping coffee and eating croissants at the open-air cafés at my leisure, strolling through museums seeing the greatest paintings and sculptures in the world, and not having a sergeant barking orders at me telling me what I can and cannot do. And so, I decided a couple of days later not to join the French Foreign Legion. A couple of weeks later, when I was back home in California, I met my future wife. It was meant to be. Yet, I have nothing but the highest respect for the French Foreign Legion, and I've had the pleasure of seeing them march in formation down the Champs-Élysées on the 14th of July, French Independence Day, a couple of times in my life while teaching overseas, and I've had the opportunity to train with French Commandos.

Now, back to the fifth paragraph of the first line of the French Foreign Legion Code of Honor. I had my boxing gloves on, and I was doing some light contact sparring with my 9-year-old nephew Gary to encourage him to be more aggressive. His father, my brother-in-law Greg, endorsed the training, and did not mind if I was a little rough with him. By this time I had already been training Gary for a couple of years, and in the last six months leading up to this day he had progressed tremendously. I mostly work on his sparring, critiqued his katas, and gave him a little dose of my Jim Wagner Reality-Based Personal Protection system.

Although Gary was being more aggressive than he had been in the past, he kept dropping his guard, and so I popped him in the face. Not hard, but enough to make it sting. I could see tears welling up inside his eyes, and I was wondering if he was going to quit or not. He stayed in there, but he had lost his edge.

Then his father said, "What's wrong Gary? Uncle Jim told you to keep your hands up."

With my rough teaching methods, coupled with the words of his father, they suddenly triggered white-hot anger within him. But Gary didn't quit; he came at me for real this time trying to hit me hard. He wanted to hurt me. He was charging in like a bull and swinging away at me hoping to land a good one on his uncle to even the score of his pain that I had caused him, which resulted in a little humiliation.

Although he came in much stronger and harder than before, the anger made his moves sloppy, and he was making more mistakes than before. His passion, or you could even say momentary "hatred," made him a less effective fighter.

I yelled at him to snap him out of it, "Gary! Quit swinging so wild. If you really want to hit me you need to focus! Block out the anger! Now really try to hit me!"

He calmed down just long enough to start being effective. Then I yelled, "Stop!" I gave him a big hug and said to him, "I'm proud of you. You are a good fighter. You just need to keep your hands up so you don't get hit." Then his father encouraged him also. It's just like I had experienced years earlier in Basic Combat Training (BCT), or "Boot Camp" as they used to called it, when I joined the United States Army; *they tear you down, only to build you back up better and stronger than before.*

The same lesson Gary learned on that day is something that every martial artist should know, and that's why I like the fifth paragraph, first line, of the French Foreign Legion Code of Honor. You don't want to be euphoric (passion) when you fight, and you don't want to be filled with anger (hate), for either one of these emotions will cloud your judgment in combat. To be effective in a fight you must be focused on effectiveness much like a shark, lion, or serpent going after their prey. How many times has somebody's anger led him or her into a fight where they were destroyed? How many times have people thought that they were invincible only to be cut down? When you engage in combat, especially in a life and death fight, you had better keep a clear head. One of France's most elite units knows this.

Training for a violent world.

These French commandos are teaching a group of people what it would be like if they were taken hostage by terrorists in a foreign country. I had the privilege of observing their training before they handed off their students to me to train.

I know, the 31 days flew by. It's hardly enough time to be wise when it comes to personal protection, and you're naturally a little disappointed that the information has ended rather abruptly.

The truth is, this book was only the beginning of your journey to obtain warrior wisdom. I have hundreds of techniques, tactics, training methods, and tidbits of information yet to share with you. Therefore, this is not the "end," end. It is only the end of your first month.

Warrior Wisdom 2 takes you through your second month of obtaining what you need to survive "a violent world." In the introduction of the second book you'll learn some more about my diverse tactical background, and you'll get 31 more days of life-saving knowledge.

FOR POLICE, MILITARY, BODYGUARDS, PRIVATE SECURITY, BOUNCERS, PRISON GUARDS, MARTIAL ARTISTS, and even BEGINNERS

WARRIOR WISDOM 2

IN ONE MONTH

ARRANGED IN DAILY READINGS

JIM WAGNER

Training for a violent world.

JIM WAGNER

REALITY-BASED
PERSONAL PROTECTION

If you'd like more information about my system,
receive training, or you are interested in
having me speak to your organization or group about
personal protection then visit my website:

www.jimwagnerrealitybased.com

NOTES

NOTES

Made in the USA
Middletown, DE
07 July 2019